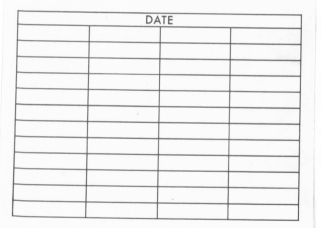

HOW TO BUILD A
HOT TUB

HOW TO BUILD A
HOT TUB

BY CARLTON HOLLANDER

Sterling Publishing Co., Inc. New York
Oak Tree Press Co., Ltd London & Sydney

Other Books of Interest

Carpentry for Beginners
Carpentry for Builders
Complete Book of Masonry, Cement, and Brickwork
Country Comforts
Handyman's Primer
How to Build a Sauna
In Harmony with Nature
Wood Decks: Construction and Maintenance

Copyright © 1981 by Carlton Hollander
Published by Sterling Publishing Co., Inc.
Two Park Avenue, New York, N.Y. 10016
Distributed in Australia by Oak Tree Press Co., Ltd.,
P.O. Box J34, Brickfield Hill, Sydney 2000, N.S.W.
Distributed in the United Kingdom by Ward Lock Ltd.
116 Baker Street, London W.1
Manufactured in the United States of America
All rights reserved
Library of Congress Catalog Card No.: 80-52332
Sterling ISBN 0-8069-0212-4 Trade   Oak Tree 7061-2741-2
              0-8069-0213-2 Library   7061-2804-4 Paper
              0-8069-8948-3 Paper

Dedication

Many thanks to Marsha, Lance, Nick, and Sean; to Marilyn, Wendy, and Randy; and to Cindy and Glynn.

Acknowledgments

The author and publishers would like to thank the following for the photographs used in this book: American Solar Energy System, California Cooperage, California Hottub, German Information Center, Bruce Hanna, Italian Government Travel Office, Japan National Tourist Organization, G. Madigan, Michael Oriti, and Redwood in the Round.

Contents

Cooperage—an Art

This book is designed to provide the information you need to build a hot tub. By constructing your tub following the instructions in this book, you will be working in an art form known as "cooperage."

Cooperage is simply the craft of building a tub or barrel without the use of glue or nails. It is also an extremely pleasurable and yes, sensual, way of handling and using wood. Coopers have practiced their skills throughout the centuries, erecting wine vats and barrels for the storage of everything from grain to whiskies. Their tools are relatively simple—a rub-

Illus. 1. The location of this outdoor tub with bench and decking offers quick and easy access to the house for those wishing instant shelter upon leaving the tub.

11

ber mallet, a saw, and measuring devices. Their raw material includes wood for the staves, iron or steel for the hoops, and an instinct and talent for making a perfect circle from squared-off pieces of wood. As you progress through the various stages involved in coopering, you will most likely find yourself developing an appreciation for the craftsmanship involved.

The professional cooper possesses an uncanny ability to cut just the right angles, feel out a circle, and knock staves into position so that they will fit perfectly. I have watched coopers work on the docks in San Pedro, California. Theirs is a skill honed by years of experience and an almost cosmic relationship with the wood and the metal hoops. Broken barrels coming off the ships docking in San Pedro are given to the coopers who, with a simple stroke of their mallets, are able to bring an errant stave back into position within a perfect circle. It is a difficult and ingenious process, one that takes patience as well as skill. But once you have successfully hammered a stave, you will feel nothing but pride in your ability to duplicate this ancient craft.

This book provides you not only with a step-by-step guide to coopering your tub, but it also includes sections dealing with foundations, locations, and the support systems which you will want to add to your tub. I have also included a chapter on the ready-made kits being offered by a number of hot-tub manufacturers (see page 115). These kits may serve the needs of those who remain somewhat skeptical about their ability to cooper a tub. If you are not accustomed to working with wood, and do not possess the basic skills of carpentry, you might be better off checking into the preassembled kits.

Any man or woman possessing average manual skills can cooper a tub. You will save money by building it yourself, but more than that, you will enjoy the pride of accomplishment—and that always makes the extra effort worthwhile!

The Tub

LOCATION

Most people who construct their own hot tub will want to lay a permanent cement foundation for their tub to rest on. In doing this, you are committing yourself to a permanent location, one which you might want to improve upon later by adding decking and other accessories. Your initial choice of a location, then, must be the best and most efficient one you can possibly make. To insure a prime location within your property boundaries, there are a number of basic, common-sense considerations on the following pages which you should take into account that will add significantly to the enjoyment of your hot tub.

Illus. 2. Before installing your hot tub on a hill, check the type of soil lying downhill, to determine if it may be susceptible to soil erosion.

The Land

Most suburbanites live on rather flat land which is basically a composition soil. For most of these people, the land will present no problem, since the concrete foundation will be essentially the same as the foundation which rests beneath the house, or which is found on a patio. However, the hills and the seashore can present land problems, as those who have suffered property erosion in the southern California mountains over the past few years will attest. Here, prior to laying a foundation, it would be wise to check with the original geological surveys of your property. These surveys are available through local departments of building and safety, where inspection reports are on file. If your property is on a hillside, it is imperative to check the type of soil lying downhill and attempt to determine whether or not it is landfill, granite, or soil strengthened by chaparral. Soil erosion can be a real problem on a hill, especially with the drainage problems inherent with a hot tub.

In coastal areas, the same considerations should be given to the kind of soil and rock on which you will be placing your tub. The continuous landslides in Malibu, California, should be warning enough to those who live on coastal land to check out soil conditions thoroughly before making any additions on their property.

Generally, the installment of a hot tub will present no more problem than laying in a patio, insofar as the soil goes. The easiest and most effective way to make certain your property can handle the strain of the foundation and the tub is to check with your local building bureau.

Natural Choices

The hot-tub experience provides year-round pleasure. Prior to deciding on a location, therefore, you should take into consideration the natural elements.

The first consideration should be the sun. Some people prefer the cooling shade of trees over their tubs, since the waters are extremely hot and the contrast provides for a refreshing experience. Others prefer the dual heat created by the sun hitting directly on the hot water in the tub. If shade is your goal, you should make a diagram of your yard and the trees within it. Then, you should draw a facsimile of the sun's path throughout its yearly cycle. If you are tracing this path in wintertime, remember that the sun's path moves farther north as we approach the summer solstice. The shifts in the sun's path diagrammed in this manner will enable you to decide

16

on the perfect location for your tub—one that will, hopefully, give the most shade throughout the year. Just remember that the sun is never in the same position from one day to the next. By studying the sun's path you can even arrange for the tub to have shade in the summer, and direct sunlight during the colder winter months.

If you prefer the lush and natural overhang of trees above your tub, keep in mind that trees change with the seasons, too. During the fall months, you may have more leaves than water in your tub. Other seasons may provide you with all kinds of tree products, from acorns to sap drippings. Of course, birds love to hang out in trees and could provide a messy problem. Check the kind of tree which your tub will rest under and learn the potentials of that tree for creating problems. It may save you from some embarrassing moments later on.

Illus. 3. Some people prefer the cooling shade of trees above their tubs. Remember, though, that many of the leaves and other natural droppings from a tree will also end up in your tub.

Of all things to consider before deciding on location, one of the most important is scenery. If you are fortunate enough to live on land that affords a view, you will most certainly want to take advantage of your natural setting by positioning your tub accordingly. There is nothing sweeter on a cool afternoon than sinking into a bubbling tub and watching the waves break on the shore, or spending an evening glorying in the sight of a city's twinkling lights. The simplest way to make sure you have the best view is to walk around your yard, stopping at various points, then squatting down and imagining yourself in a tub. You'll know when you've found the right spot! Believe it or not, I've seen tubs in the hills of southern California that sat next to huge oak trees, where a spot only 5 feet (1.52 m) to either side would have offered bathers a spectacular view of the Los Angeles basin. When asked about the odd location of his tub, one owner merely shrugged and grinned sheepishly. He had made a mistake, and it would have involved major expense, as well as trouble, to correct it.

The suburbanite whose yard is surrounded by concrete blocks or wood fences should not be depressed about his lack of a view. With a little imagination, and a green thumb, a beautiful and natural environment can be created in any corner of any yard. The hot tub is a natural and sensual experience, and the addition of plants and shrubbery around the tub will add immensely to that experience.

City-dwellers have developed their own unique style for fitting a hot tub into their lives (see Illus. 4). The determined large-city hot-tub enthusiast may lack the natural surroundings of trees or an ocean view, but a metropolitan skyline seen from the top of a high-rise building offers a spectacular view of a different sort.

Groups of hot tubbers known as *purists* demand an entirely natural setting for their soaks. In California, there are many small groups of enthusiasts who have banded together and built tubs on a cooperative basis. One member of the group donates a piece of land, preferably land that is secluded and untouched by human hands. The hot tub is placed on the land and shared by the members of the group whenever they desire a soak. For those who are accustomed to living communally, the co-op tub works quite well. For most of us, however, the co-op, no matter how beautiful the setting, makes for more problems and social confrontations than it is worth.

Dealing with the elements of Mother Nature is never easy. She's always more than willing to throw a few curves into the best-laid plans of hot tubbers. In recent years, we have all grown accustomed to strange shifts in the weather patterns, and the inability to count on its cycles to remain consistent. Nonetheless, like the weatherman, you should make an effort to

California Hottub

Illus. 4. Some New Yorkers have adapted the hot tub to their own unique scenery. City or country, hot or cold climate, every home can fit a hot tub.

judge conditions in your area by doing a little research into former patterns. Being aware of cold northerlies, or certain freakish phenomena like southern California's Santa Ana winds, will allow you to locate your tub in an appropriate spot. Although some people love the bracing cold when they emerge from the hot waters of a tub, almost everyone dislikes a hard-edged wind. So, it would be wise to give some thought to weather variations in your area and to position your tub accordingly for the ideal location.

Hot tubbing is becoming increasingly popular in colder climates. The Finns have long cherished their ritual of hot bathing and then running into an ice-cold lake or just rolling around in the snow. Many hot tubbers share the Finns' enthusiasm for these drastic changes in temperature. So, if hot tubbing and snow appeal to you, make certain that you place your tub in a position where you will have easy access to snow in the winter. Also,

California Cooperage

Illus. 5. If you want to follow the robust example of the Finns and roll around in the snow after bathing in hot water, make sure to locate your tub where you'll have easy access to winter snow. Winterizing kits are available to allow use of hot tubs in freezing climates.

in the colder climates, you will definitely have to take wind conditions into account. Use already existing shelters, such as a house or a fence, or erect your own windscreens, to insure year-round use of your tub.

The natural setting of your tub is vitally important to the enjoyment you will receive from it. Hot tubbing brings the bather closer to his or her environment, and putting thought into the selection of that environment pays off in extremely pleasurable dividends.

Drainage

Most people who have hot tubs also have filtering systems which keep the water clean. Even so, it is necessary periodically to drain the tub and to clean it. How often you must drain and clean depends on how often you use the tub, the kinds of chemicals you put into the water, and other considerations. When you plan the location of your tub, then, remember that hundreds of gallons of water will be unleashed from the tub during draining. Common sense will dictate how and where your tub will be best located for drainage. Most tubs are raised on a foundation and platform, and drainage is accomplished through the natural forces of gravity. Many tubbers like to use the water from their tubs to irrigate their gardens. This is done simply by attaching a hose to your drain and pulling the plug, directing the flow of water to those areas where it is needed. This is by far the most economical and conservation-minded way of draining your tub.

Make certain when you select your location that drainage will not seep back into the foundation of your home or a nearby structure. Also, if you are on a hill, check the flow from your tub with your neighbors' homes in mind. Flooding your neighbors' yards with hot-tub water can make you an overnight blight on the neighborhood.

Privacy

Many hot-tub enthusiasts insist that hot tubbing offers a natural incentive for people to take off their clothes. It is a fact that a majority of hot tubbing is done in the nude, and the purists are the first to tell you that a swimsuit only hinders the natural feeling of a soak. Of course, what you wear is up to you. Swimsuits or not, however, privacy when tubbing is essential to a good experience. People in a tub tend to open up and relax, feeling somewhat isolated from the hassles and problems of the everyday world. Curious neighbors or passersby peering in at you while you try to shake off the angst of the 20th century is not what hot tubbing is all about.

Think about privacy not only when planning your tub's location, but also in terms of access to the tub from the house. If you and your friends enjoy nude bathing, you will want to make certain that the access routes to your tub are protected. Also, many people who enjoy the tub also enjoy sunbathing afterwards, or just walking around in the cool night air between soaks. It is not against the law to be naked in your own backyard, but people are people, and a horde of nude bodies is almost certain to draw a crowd.

There are, of course, many ways to insure privacy—fencing or the strategic positioning of shrubbery are two methods that will work just fine. One hot tub I visited in south Pasadena, California was enclosed on three sides by 8-foot-(2.44-m-) high redwood fencing, with the open side looking out on a majestic valley. This construction worked well for shielding bathers against vile weather, for taking advantage of the spectacular

Illus. 6. Strategically placed fencing around a tub will ensure privacy from curious spectators. Leave one or two sides open for scenic views.

(Right) Illus. 7. The more elaborate fencing pictured here lends an almost indoors atmosphere to the open porch location of this tub.

(Below) Illus. 8. This fencing not only ensures privacy, but it is also attractive.

view, and for insuring privacy. The redwood fencing extended 20 feet (6.10 m) between the house and the tub, guaranteeing bathers complete privacy to and from the tub.

Privacy is a matter of personal style, but keep in mind that not everyone feels the same way about their body as you may about yours. With a little extra effort, you will be able to provide a comfortable and pleasant surrounding for everyone, regardless of their particular inhibitions.

The Functions of Your Tub

Before you commit yourself to a location, give some thought as to how you are going to use your new tub. Will you be throwing parties every weekend with hordes of enthusiasts swarming into your tub? Or, will the tub serve just yourself and a special friend? The kind of person you are, and the type of social life you would like to develop around your tub will most definitely affect choice of location.

One Hollywood screenwriter I know uses his small hot tub just for himself and his wife. The tub is placed just outside his bedroom and is accessible through a sliding glass door. For his purposes, the location is perfect. Another gentleman enjoys throwing hot-tub parties, and has placed his large tub in the middle of his yard, with plenty of decking surrounding it. The tub is always the center of his parties, with guests soaking or lounging on the deck. It makes for an exceptional social hub.

Hot tubs are being used increasingly by the elderly. The soak alleviates many of the ills of old age, and is a blessing to those suffering from muscle and bone disorders. If you are planning to use your tub for health purposes, make certain you place the tub in an accessible location. I would suggest keeping it fairly close to the house, allowing the bather instant shelter when he or she emerges from the tub. Also, consider the problems of getting into the tub, and select a location that would precipitate easy access by way of a raised deck or a good ladder. This rule applies not only to the elderly and the infirm, but, generally, to everyone. Most of us are long past the point where we can easily execute a vault into a 4-foot- (1.22-m-) high tub.

Once you have decided on the location of your tub, and have laid the foundation for it, it would be somewhat difficult to move it. Therefore, think about the possibility of installing decking and other accessories in the future, and make sure that your location will allow you to add to your tub as you go along. If, for instance, you have a patio in your yard and intend someday to build a stepped decking around your tub, make certain that the tub is far enough away from the patio so that you do not have to use patio space for your decking. Or, if you decide to place your tub in a corner of the yard, keep it far enough away from the fences so that you and your guests will be able to enter and lounge around the tub from all sides. As most people have discovered, once a tub becomes part of their lives, it is most difficult for them not to make it a center of their pleasure environment. For some people, the hot tub alone is enough, but most hot-tub owners will add decking and other additions at some time or another. So, consider what you might want to do with your tub in the future and locate your tub accordingly.

Illus. 9. Decking doesn't have to be expensive or elaborate. This simple above-ground tub with a minimal floor base, stairs, deck, and fencing, offers all the conveniences you need to enjoy a hot tub. A small tub offers the additional benefit of being quick and inexpensive to heat up.

Conclusion

Location of your tub is purely a matter of choice, but you should be aware of a few important factors regarding your tub and your property before deciding on where to place it. First, the tub will become something of a permanent fixture in your yard. You will find that much of your social life will revolve around the tub, and, like a swimming pool, it will become a popular gathering place. Incorporate your tub into your environment, using all the natural benefits of your space to enhance the environment of the tub. Remember, the tub is designed for pleasure.

The addition of a hot tub in a natural and enjoyable setting will add significantly to the value of your home and property. Any investment that you can make to enhance the setting and improve the conditions around your tub will add considerably to your financial equity. The dividends from a well-placed tub will come in the form of money as well as pleasure. Keep in mind that the location of your tub is a primary ingredient to the total success of your hot-tub experience. Give it serious thought before you begin the actual construction and laying of the foundation.

Illus. 10. The elaborate design of this hot-tub environment adds significantly to the value of the owner's home and property.

CONSTRUCTION

There are three major steps involved in the building of a hot tub. The first step is the laying of the foundation, the second is the actual construction of your tub, and the third is the inclusion of your heating, pumping, and filtering systems.

Not all the steps and directions which follow are necessary, but they are advisable. For instance, some people do not use a concrete foundation beneath their tub, preferring instead to set the tub on railroad ties. Other people do not use filters, but drain and clean their tubs manually. There are purists within the hot-tub community who disdain the use of machinery when a strong arm will do just as well. Decisions about how extensive you will want your system to be are, of course, up to you. What we will propose is a complete and functional hot-tub system that should satisfy your needs, one that functions with the least amount of hassle and work once the tub is completed. Should you choose to eliminate some steps along the way, it would be advisable to check with others who have done the same and learn how their alternatives worked out.

The Foundation

The average "large" tub is 6 feet (1.83 m) in diameter and 4 feet (1.22 m) high. Thus, your foundation must be large enough for the tub to sit on. The "average" square which you will want to construct is a foundation of 36 square feet (10.8 m²), or 6 feet (1.83 m) on each side.

Some people do not use a concrete foundation, but prefer to rest their tub directly on the ground, using the large chine joists beneath the floorboards for support. A solid concrete foundation, however, is inexpensive and relatively easy to construct, and will most certainly save you the heartbreak of a tub rotting because of vegetation growing underneath, mud creeping into the floorboards, and other disasters which a good foundation can prevent. So, with all possible emphasis, we urge you to lay a concrete foundation.

The job is a simple one. Once you have chosen your spot, clear the land of rocks, shrubs and other paraphernalia that will disrupt your concrete pour. Stake out the area on which you will lay your foundation by approximating the corners, driving in wooden stakes or large nails, and running a string around the circumference of your square. At this time, you should review your positioning from all angles and make your final aesthetic considerations. If you are satisfied with your position and scenery, then you are ready to begin.

Since the hot tub will be resting upon the cement in a free-form state—that is, the tub's geometric perfection will not be contingent upon the perfection of your foundation—it is not necessary to pour a perfect square with perfect right angles at the corners. Your tub will simply rest on this block, secured, if you so desire, by anchor bolts (more about this later, as we pour the concrete). Your foremost consideration when pouring the foundation will be to make sure that the surface is level. Since water always retains a perfect level, any variation or slant in your foundation will show up in the hot tub.

To pour a 36-square-foot- (10.8-m²-) foundation, you will need four 2 × 4's, each 6 feet (1.83 m) in length. These will provide the frame for the pouring of the cement, and need not be high quality lumber. The cheaper the better—just make sure that the top edges are not gutted or uneven, since you will be using these surfaces to plane down the cement.

Cut two pieces of lumber down to 5 feet 6 inches (1.67 m). Lay these two pieces opposite one another, then line up the 6-footers (1.83 m) against them, with the shorter pieces inside (see Illus. 11). Nail the ends

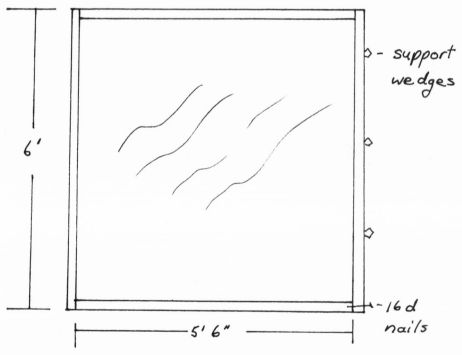

Illus. 11. Top view of the foundation frame using four 2 x 4's, two 6 feet (1.83 m) long and two 5 feet 6 inches (1.67 m) long. Nail the ends together with 16d nails, leaving the heads sticking out so you can disassemble the frame later. Drive support pegs on the outer edge of the foundation in order to secure its position during the pouring and levelling.

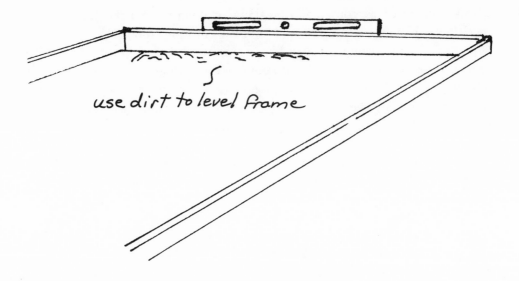

use dirt to level frame

Illus. 12. Before pouring the cement, use a carpenter's level to make sure that your frame is level. Pack dirt beneath the frame to raise it, or remove dirt to lower it.

together, using 16d nails, leaving the heads sticking out since you will disassemble the frame once the cement has hardened. Now, move your frame into place, using the string as a guide. Remove the string and the stakes. One suggestion at this time would be to drive support pegs on the outer edge of the foundation in order to secure its position during the pouring and levelling. These will keep the foundation from shifting. Use 4- or 6-inch (10.16–15.24-cm) wooden stakes, securing the corners with one stake in the center of each side.

Prior to pouring your cement, you should consider whether or not you want to insert anchor bolts. If you do, obviously you must have the bolts on hand during the pouring and put them in place before the cement dries. The anchor bolts can be used later to secure decking, or to fasten a ladder to the foundation. Even if you have no plans for accessories at the present time, it is advisable to put the bolts in. It's much simpler than drilling into the cement later on.

The last step in readying the frame for the pouring of cement is to make sure that it is level. Use a carpenter's level, checking each side and the corners. The easiest method of levelling off the frame is to pack dirt beneath the frame where you need to raise it, or remove dirt when it is necessary to lower it (see Illus. 12). Some carpenters will use wooden wedges to

29

raise or lower their frame, but dirt works just as effectively in this case. Re-check your levels as you adjust the frame, making certain that all sides are perfect. Now, you are ready to pour your cement foundation.

Some people do not like working with cement, and prefer to hire a professional to come in and pour the foundation. Although this job is not terrifically expensive, you can save more money by pouring it yourself. You can also enjoy the satisfaction of doing the job from start to finish. The easiest and simplest method of pouring cement is to use the ready-mix cement sold at all lumber and department stores. This cement already has rocks in it, and saves you the step of mixing them into the cement. All you need to do is add water, mix it all up in a wheelbarrow, and you are ready to pour.

Cement is sold by the bag, and one bag will fill two-thirds of a cubic foot ($.02m^3$). If you are pouring a foundation that measures 6 feet (1.83 m) on a side, and you are using 2 × 4's for your frame, your cubic foot measurement will be calculated by multiplying the length by the width by the depth. In this case, 6 × 6 × ⅓ (1.83 m × 1.83 m × 10.16 cm) [4 inches (10.16 cm) equalling one-third of a foot]. Thus, you will need approximately 12 cubic feet ($.36 \text{ m}^3$) of cement. That should be a minimum figure, since parts of your foundation will be over 4 inches (10.16 cm) in depth due to the fact that your land is not totally level. In those places where you have raised your frame to level it off, measure the differential and calculate those extra inches (millimeters) in depth when figuring your cubic feet. For our purposes, let's assume that the frame rests without deviation, and that we do have 12 cubic feet ($.36 \text{ m}^3$) to pour. Divide 12 cubic feet ($.36 \text{ m}^3$) by ⅔ and you will arrive at the number of bags you need. Your salesman will help with this figure, probably suggesting that you get one extra bag for good measure. So, for our purposes, you will need 18 bags plus that extra bag, for a total of 19. Prices in Los Angeles for the ready-mix cement ranged from $2.50 to $3.00 per bag in 1980.

To pour your foundation, you will need a wheelbarrow, a trowel, a 2 × 6 piece of lumber at least 6 feet (1.83 m) in length, water, and a shovel. Do not attempt to pour your cement on a rainy day, since the added water will destroy the proper mix of your cement. A mist or light drizzle doesn't present a problem. If you can, invite a friend over to help you. Once you begin pouring, you will have to stay with the job until you are finished. Cement dries unevenly, with the surface crusting while the interior stays mushy. While you mix in the wheelbarrow, your friend should concentrate on moving the cement to the corners and edges of the frame, then working it back into the center (see Illus. 13). This will help speed up

Illus. 13. Pour cement to the corners and edges of the frame first, then work it back towards the center. Turn the cement over to keep the rocks as far beneath the surface as possible.

the pour, and will lessen any chance of your having to work with crusting cement. Turn the cement over to keep the rocks as far beneath the surface as possible. Otherwise, they will hamper the effectiveness of smoothing down the surface when you have finished.

Once the frame is filled with cement, use the 6-foot (1.83-m) 2 × 6 to scrape off the excess surface cement (see Illus. 14). With you holding one end, and your friend holding the other, simply pull the wood across the surface, angling it as you go, until the surface is level with the top of your foundation. Now you can begin troweling, using a cement trowel. A professional makes troweling look easy, moving in a circular motion across

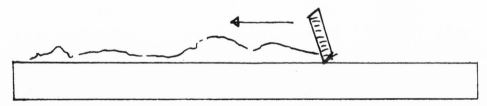

Illus. 14. When the frame is filled with cement, use the 6-foot (1.83-m) 2 x 6 to scrape off the excess surface cement.

31

the surface, magically smoothing out the cement. If you have never trow-eled before, you will discover that it is not as easy as it appears. Pitting of the cement is a common problem caused by placing the trowel too flat on the surface, thus causing the edge of the tool to dig in. Avoid this by angling the trowel slightly, and working in circular motions. Don't panic. You have plenty of time to smooth out your foundation, and a little experimenting with the trowel should result in a succession of masterful strokes.

Once you have smoothed down the surface, check the overall level. Don't place the level directly on the cement, but place it on a piece of cardboard to protect the foundation's surface. Remember, this is the last chance you will have to make certain that your foundation is perfectly level. Allow the cement to dry for an hour, then trowel once again. At this time, you may sink your anchor bolts. The cement should be soft enough to insert the bolts by hand, but hard enough to prevent any shifting once they're in place (see Illus. 15). Check your foundation after another hour or two, and

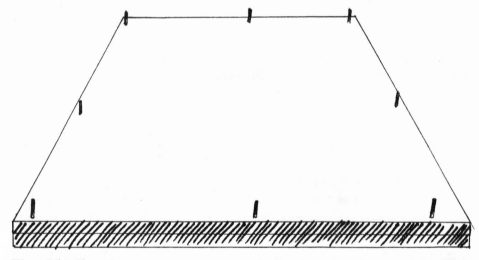

Illus. 15. Allow the cement to dry for an hour, then trowel once again. Sink your anchor bolts when the cement is still soft enough to insert the bolts by hand, but hard enough to prevent any shifting once they're in place.

smooth down any irregularities. Most cement takes 72 hours to harden com-pletely, so now you can sit back and wait. After the 72-hour period, you can remove the boards that frame the foundation. Your foundation is now complete.

Building the Tub

The initial step in constructing your tub is selecting the wood. Redwood hot tubs are the most popular for a very good reason. Kiln-dried, clear redwood is an excellent wood for your tub because it is light, easy to work with, and swells perfectly when water is added to your tub. This swelling is imperative because, initially, your tub will leak until the wood expands and closes the gaps and joints. There are other kinds of wood that will suffice for your purposes, like Douglas fir and certain cypresses. But to get the most effective and time-tested quality, you should use redwood.

The tub itself is comprised of the wall, which is made up of staves set side by side, the floor, and metal hoops encircling the staves to secure them. The most highly recommended height for a hot tub is 4 feet (1.22 m), providing for easy access with enough depth to facilitate the hot-tub experience. So, you will need a certain number of redwood staves at 4 feet (1.22 m) apiece to encircle your tub, thus forming the wall.

When purchasing your wood, you will need to buy the staves and the floorboards. The staves should be 2 × 6's, and the floorboards should be as wide as possible, 2 × 10's or 2 × 12's. Using wide floorboards decreases the chances of your floor leaking since you will have fewer joints to contend with. The floorboards should be long enough so that you will be able to inscribe a 6-foot (1.83-m) circle when they are lying side by side. Thus, if you are buying 8-foot (2.44-m) lengths at a width of 12 inches (30.48 cm), you will need approximately six pieces. However, since wood is never measured at the marketplace with total accuracy, it would be wise to pick up one extra piece.

When selecting your wood, it is imperative that you select kiln-dried wood. This type of lumber will absorb the water and expand when you fill your tub. Wood that is not dried will take in less water and not expand as much, thus retaining the initial leaks when the tub is filled. Also, select lumber that is straight and vertically grained (see Illus. 16). You can determine this by holding the wood at eye level and sighting down the length. Your lumber salesman will help with this process. The grain should be vertical, running as near perfectly as possible up and down the length. In "lumber-ese," this is called *all heart*. If you search long enough, you should have no problem finding the perfect pieces of redwood. Another important consideration. when selecting your wood is to choose pieces that are *clear*, or without knots. Knotted lumber does not work well in a hot tub simply because knots leak, and they will not expand. Some people maintain that knots which do not penetrate both sides of the wood are acceptable for a hot tub, but it

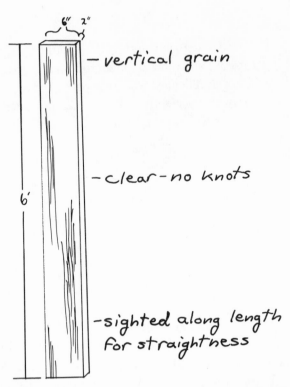

Illus. 16. Select kiln-dried lumber that is straight and vertically grained. You can determine this by holding the wood at eye level and sighting down the length. Choose pieces that are clear, without knots.

is much safer and wiser to spend a few extra minutes and find yourself perfectly clear wood.

Your selection process, therefore, will involve finding wood that has vertical grain, that is kiln dried, straight, and clear. These qualities should also be considered when selecting your floorboards.

The other lumber you will need will be four 4 × 4's or 4 × 6's which will serve as the chine joists. The chine joists will rest on the cement foundation at equal intervals, and the tub itself will rest on the joists. The wood need not be perfect, that is, you do not have to use perfectly clear or all-heart lumber. What you should remember, however, is to make certain that all your joists are exactly the same height. Your hot tub will not be level if one chine joist is higher than the other. All in all, you will need: 4 4 × 4 6-foot (1.83-m) chine joists; 7 2 × 12's over 6 feet (1.83 m) in length for the floorboards; and 45 2 × 6's at 4 feet (1.22 m) in length for the staves. Commonly accepted figures for the number of staves needed are: for a 4-foot (1.22-m) tub, 30 staves; for a 5-foot (1.52-m) tub, 37 staves; for a 6-foot (1.83-m) tub, 45 staves; and 60 staves for an 8-footer (2.44 m). The actual widths of lumber are never exact, but these figures will provide you with a reasonable estimate. The final stave will need to be modified because it will never fit perfectly. It is wise to purchase a few extra pieces of lumber for your staves. These can always be used later for constructing the benches or the ladder.

Take your 45 staves and cut them each to a length of 4 feet (1.22 m). A circular saw will suffice, but if you have access to a table jig-saw, use that. You will want each stave to be exactly the same length, and cut to a perfect right angle. Check each piece with a square, and measure each as you cut it. Uneven staves will mean a lot of extra work later on when you have to file and sand them to even off the top rim of your tub.

Once the staves are cut to the proper length, once again 4 feet (1.22 m) being a very workable and acceptable height for a hot tub, it is time to angle the edges of your staves so that when you put them side by side they will form a circle. This process is called "bevelling." Bevelling involves cutting an angle down each side of the stave so that when you view the stave from the top it forms a trapezoid (see Illus. 17). The outside wall of the tub will be formed by the longer width, and the inner wall by the shorter width.

interior

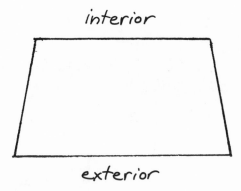

exterior

Illus. 17. Bevelling involves cutting an angle down each side of the stave so that when you view the stave from the top it forms a trapezoid. The outside wall of the tub will be formed by the longer width, and the inner wall by the shorter width.

To understand the bevelling process, simply place two of the staves side by side. You will see that they will form a straight line. Now imagine them angled, and you will see the beginning of a curve. The greater the angle, the more severe the curve. To form a certain size circle, there are absolute angles at which you must cut. For a 4-foot (1.22-m) diameter tub, you will need a 6½-degree cut; a 5-foot (1.52-m) tub demands a 5-degree 15-minute cut; and our 6-footer (1.83 m) necessitates a 4¼-degree cut.

Illus. 18. Wood from the lumber-yard is rough cut. Use a carpenter's square to make sure you cut a perfect right angle.

Illus. 19. Use a handsaw for almost any wood-cutting odd job during construction.

Illus. 20. Use a jigsaw to cut the grooves.

Illus. 21. Use a rubber mallet to knock the staves together, and for any other pounding work on the wood.

Illus. 22. Use a table saw to square off rounded edges on lumber, and to cut the staves to measurement. Make certain to cut a right angle.

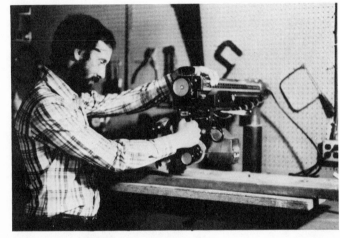

Illus. 23. Use a table saw, also, to bevel your staves. Adjust the tilt of the saw to cut the proper angle.

Use a table saw to bevel your staves. Each table saw has an adjustable angle whereby the blade may be tilted up to a 45-degree angle. What you will need (for the 6-foot [1.83-m] tub) is an angle of 4 degrees, 15 minutes—or 4¼ degrees (see Illus. 24). Your table saw will probably have markings at 4 degrees and 5 degrees. To get the cut at exactly 4¼ degrees will most likely require the use of a protractor. Set the saw at 4 degrees, then measure with the protractor and mark where the extra quarter degree will fall. Adjust your tilt and cut again, hopefully hitting the angle squarely on the mark. This may take a few tries before you get it exactly right. Once you have fixed the angle, run all of your staves through the saw, except for the one which will be the last stave.

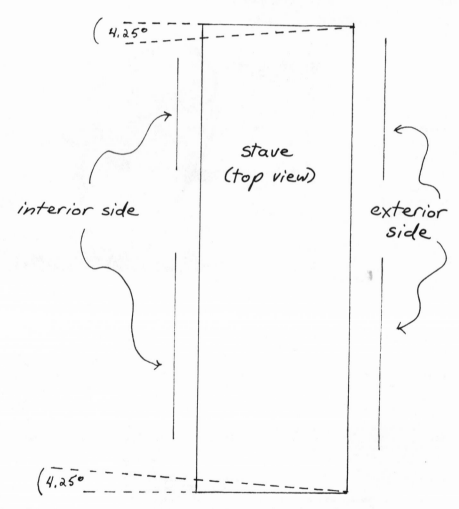

Illus. 24. Use a table saw to bevel your staves. For the 6-foot (1.83-m) tub, you will need an angle of 4 degrees 15 minutes.

For those who do not have access to a good table saw with proper cutting guides, you can, for a small amount of money, have your staves bevelled at a lumberyard. If you have any doubts about the potential of your equipment to cut the needed angle, check with a professional before cutting. Getting the angles on the staves exactly right is one of the most difficult steps in building your hot tub. Do not hesitate to call on a friend or a local professional for assistance.

Now that you have all of your staves (except the last one) angled properly so that when placed side by side they will form a 6-foot (1.83-m) circle, it is time to dado out the groove, or croze. The groove will be near the bottom of the stave, on the inside face. The staves will be attached to the floor by knocking each stave into the floor by using a cooper's mallet. The floor will thus fit it directly into your groove. The groove should be placed at least 3 inches (7.62 cm) from the bottom of the stave. It should be ¾ inch (19.05 mm) deep and 3/16 inch (4.76 mm) narrower than the thickness of the floorboards. Being thinner, the groove will create a snug fit when you pound the stave into the floor. Also, when determining exactly how thick your groove should be, measure your floorboards and never assume that the lumberyard measurements are accurate.

You will need a dado saw to cut your groove. The dado is a three-bladed saw designed to cut grooves or slots into wood. A ¾-inch (19.05-mm) dado set will cut a groove ¾ inch (19.05 mm) into your stave. To get a slot 1½ inches (3.81 cm) in width, you will need to make two separate cuts (see Illus. 25). Once you have installed your dado, adjust the depth to ⅝ inch (15.88 mm) and run your cutting jig through, thus grooving a slot. This will allow you to place your staves next to the jig and make a clean cut without running into the surface of the jig itself. Next, measure 3 inches (7.62 cm) from the right of the dado and draw a straight line abso-

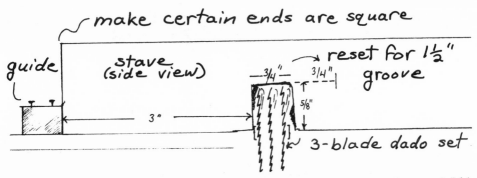

Illus. 25. Use a dado saw to cut a groove ⅝ inch (15.88 mm) deep and 1½ inches (3.81 cm) wide. The groove should begin 3 inches (7.62 mm) from the bottom of the stave.

39

lutely perpendicular to the jig. Nail down a piece of wood, leaving the nails exposed for easy movement later. Now, you have your right-handed guide. Place the stave against your guide, with the inside face down, and run it through the dado. You should now have a groove ⅝ inch (15.88 mm) deep and ¾ inch (19.05 mm) wide, and one which begins exactly 3 inches (7.62 mm) from the bottom of the stave. Groove all 45 staves in this manner, then reset the position of your right-handed guide ¾ inch (19.05 mm) farther to the right. Repeat the dado cut, and you will have all staves with a groove that is 1½ inches (3.81 cm) wide and ⅝ inch (15 mm) deep (see Illus. 26).

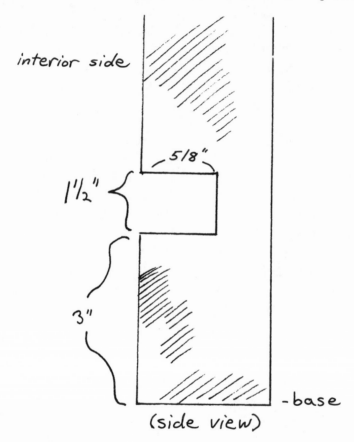

Illus. 26. All forty-five staves should now have a groove 1½ inches (3.81 cm) wide and ⅝ inch (15 mm) deep.

Using a file, clean out the grooves and remove the rough edges and excess splinters.

You now have 45 staves ready to attach to the floor of your tub. It is a good idea at this time to make certain that all your staves are exactly the same height, that the angles are correct, and that the grooves are exactly

40

the same distance from the bottom and are of an equal width. The last stave, grooved at this time but without angles, should also be examined for height and the location of the groove. This stave will have to be specially cut to fit snugly into the gap when all the other staves are in place. There is no sure way that you can predetermine the proper angle for this piece. You will have to do that as the last step in staving your hot tub. Store your staves in a dry place to avoid contact with water and premature expansion.

The Floor

You will need seven floorboards, 2 × 12's, each at least 6 feet (1.83 m) in length. In preparing the boards, you should make certain that their edges are perfectly squared off. Wood tends to be rounded at the edges, but by pulling each of the boards through a table saw, you can square them off so you will have a perfectly square edge (see Illus. 27). This step will make certain that there are no gaps for leaks when the boards are placed side by side for the floor.

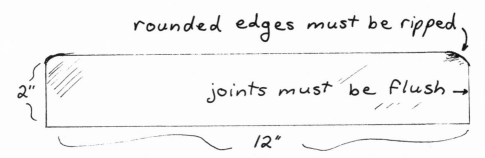

Illus. 27. For the floor, you'll need seven 2 x 12 boards, each at least 6 feet (1.83 m) long. Pull each board through a table saw to square off the edges.

To put the floorboards together, you will have to dowel them together. Dowelling is a process whereby pegs are placed into holes, and the floor pieces are attached by joining these pegs. If you dowel properly, you avoid having to use glue or waterproof mastic to hold the boards together. If you decide to use a waterproof mastic, however, make certain that when joining the boards you apply the mastic to the lower sections of the floorboards so that it will not seep up through the joints and create a slick inside the tub. Mastic by itself is not really enough to hold the tub together, so you should also dowel.

Lay the floorboards side by side, then mark where you will want to drill the holes. The best placement is to drill one hole in the center, and one on either end, 3 or 4 inches (7.62–10.16 cm) from the end. The best way to dowel is to use a dowelling jig, a clamp that attaches to the boards

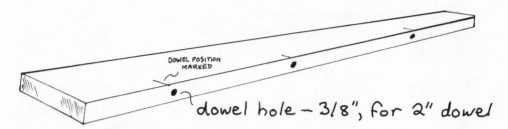

dowel hole – 3/8", for 2" dowel

Illus. 28. You will have to dowel the floorboards together. Drill one hole in the center of each board and one on either end, 3 or 4 inches (7.62–10.16 cm) from the end. Use 2-inch (50–mm) dowels that are ⅜ inch (9.53 mm) in diameter and drill the holes accordingly.

and guarantees a bore that is precise every time. Use 2-inch (50-mm) dowels that are ⅜ inch (9.53 mm) in diameter and drill your holes accordingly (see Illus. 28). Use a rubber mallet to tap the dowels into place. Then, place your

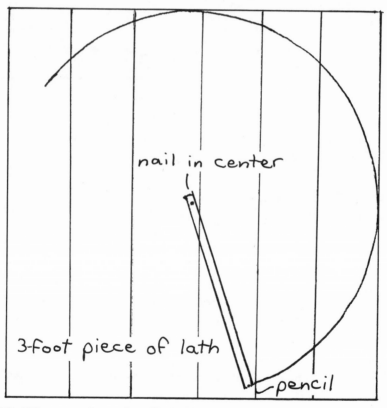

nail in center

3-foot piece of lath

pencil

Illus. 29. When you have dowelled all seven floorboards together, inscribe a circle with a radius of 3 feet (91.44 cm). Drill a hole for a pencil in one end of a 3-foot-long (91.44–cm) piece of lath. Find the center of the floor, and tack the lath into it. With your homemade compass, draw a 6-foot (1.83–m) circle.

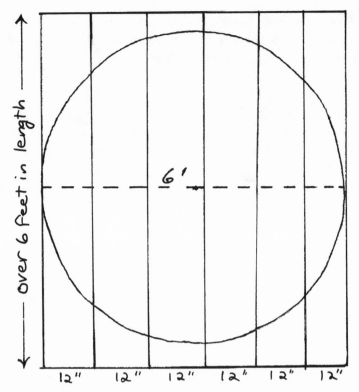

over 6 feet in length

6'

12" 12" 12" 12" 12" 12"

Illus. 30. Use a saber saw to cut your circle out, following the line you drew with your homemade compass. When you begin your cut, stay just at the outer edge of your pencilled line and work slowly, following the curve.

floorboards on a pair of sawhorses and slide each board up against the next, lining up the dowels. Use the mallet to tap the boards gently together. If you are going to be using a mastic, you should apply it at this time.

Once you have dowelled all seven boards together, keep your floor on the sawhorses. The next step is to cut a circle. Since your tub will be 6 feet (1.83 m) in diameter, you will be inscribing a circle with a radius of 3 feet (91.44 cm) (see Illus. 29). Use a piece of lath that is 3 feet (91.44 cm) long and drill a hole in one end of it for a pencil. Then find the center of the floor. This point does not have to be exact as long as there is enough floor to scribe a circle that is 6 feet (1.83 m) in diameter (see Illus. 30). Nail the end of the lath into the center point, using a tack so that you do not puncture the wood. Now, with the pencil at the far end, you have a homemade compass. Draw your circle until you have a sharp and defined line to follow when you begin sawing.

Sawing a circle is not easy work. It takes patience and the proper tool. The saber saw is the proper tool to use, since it is designed for cutting circles. When you begin your cut, stay just at the outer edge of your pencilled line and work slowly, following the curve. If you are borrowing or renting a saw, explain to the owner what you are going to be doing and he will show you how to angle the blade to compensate for the outward pull of the saw.

Hopefully, you will cut a perfect 6-foot (1.83-m) floor. To keep the boards secure while moving the floor, tack three strips of lath across the floor, and across the joints (see Illus. 31). Next, take a plane or sander and bevel the edges of the floor to facilitate attaching the staves. A slightly angled edge will make it easier to pound on the staves and guarantees a better fit. At this point, you should be viewing the top of the floor, or the smooth bottom of the tub. Turn the floor over, and you will be ready to attach the chine joists.

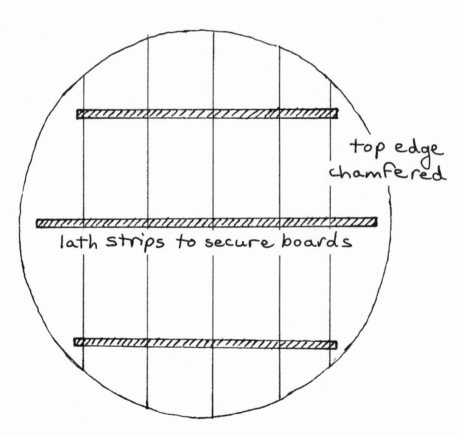

Illus. 31. To keep the boards secure while moving the floor, tack three strips of lath across the floor, and across the joints.

The Chine Joists

The chine joists will be construction-grade 4 × 4 redwoods. They will be placed perpendicular to the joints of the floorboard, and will provide for the base of the hot tub. The chine joists will also raise the bottom of the tub some 4 inches (10.16 cm) off your concrete foundation, thus serving to maintain circulation beneath the tub. This will prevent the bottom of the tub from becoming moist and eventually suffering from mold and warp.

The chine joists should be placed about 18 inches (45.72 cm) apart, measuring from the center of each joist. This measurement will give you equal strength and support across the floor, since the diameter of your floor is 72 inches (182.88 cm), or four times 18 (see Illus. 32). After laying out the chine joists, pencil in their positions. Now, measure where you will want to cut them at each end—about 3 inches (7.62 cm) in from the edge of the floor is fine. Mark your cut and saw off the ends. Now, place the chine joists back in position and toenail them into position using 6d nails so that the point of the nail will not protrude to the other side. Toenail them at a 45-degree angle, using four to five nails for each side of each chine joist

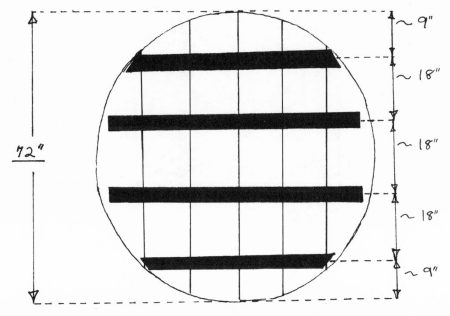

Illus. 32. Place the 4 x 4 chine joists about 18 inches (45.72 cm) apart, and perpendicular to the joints of the floorboards. This will give equal strength and support across the floor.

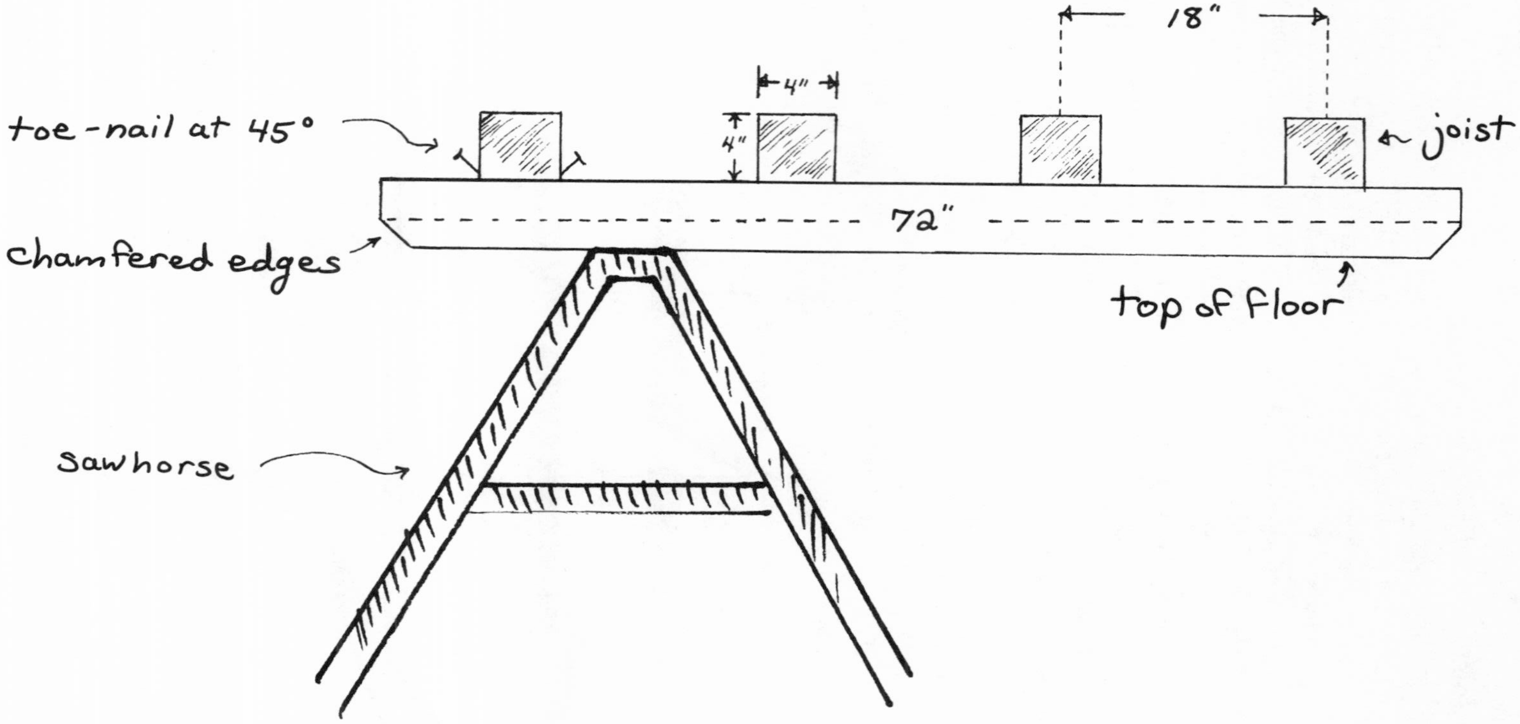

Illus. 33. With the floorboards still wrong-side-up on the sawhorses, toenail the chine joists into position, using 6d nails, at a 45-degree angle.

(see Illus. 33). Now, you are ready to turn your floor over. Leave the lath strips on to secure the boards as you attach the staves. At this time, you may move your floor into position on the foundation.

While the floor is completely exposed, you might want to consider drilling the hole for the drain (see page 60). It is easier to do this work now instead of crawling into the tub later on when the staves are in position.

Staving

Place the first stave into position between two of the floorboards, with the joint midpoint at the stave. Line the groove up with the floorboard, then tap in the stave with the heel of your hand and then with a rubber mallet (see Illus. 34). Do this gently and tap the stave in only halfway. If the stave leans out too far, brace it with a piece of lath (see Illus. 35).

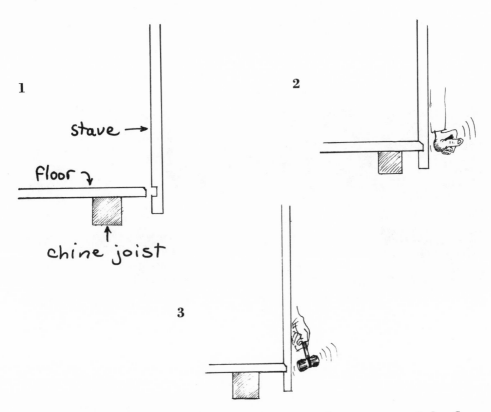

Illus. 34 (1) Place the first stave into position between two of the floorboards, with the joint midpoint at the stave. Line the groove up with the floorboard. (2) Gently tap in the stave with the heel of your hand, and then (3) with a rubber mallet. Tap the stave in only halfway.

47

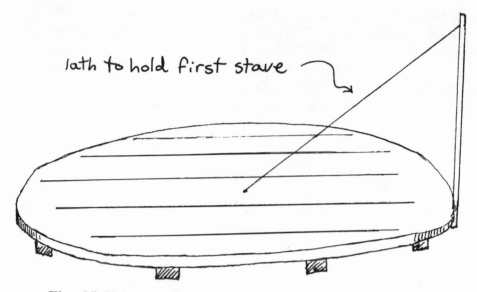

lath to hold first stave

Illus. 35. If the stave leans out too far, brace it with a piece of lath.

Next, begin placing one stave next to the other and securing them to the floorboard. As each stave is mounted, hit the edge of it and drive it snugly against the other staves (see Illus. 36). Continue to do this as you

California Cooperage

Illus. 36. As each stave is mounted on the floorboard, hit the edge of it with a rubber mallet and drive it snugly against the other staves. Continue to do this as you work your way around the tub, closing the gaps as firmly as possible.

48

work your way around the tub, closing the gaps as firmly as possible. After you have pounded the first two staves in, go back and pound the original stave as far as you can into the floor. Do this with the second stave, and then with each stave as you progress. Use duct or electrical tape to secure the tops of the staves against one another as you work your way around. This will keep them from shifting while you work (see Illus. 37).

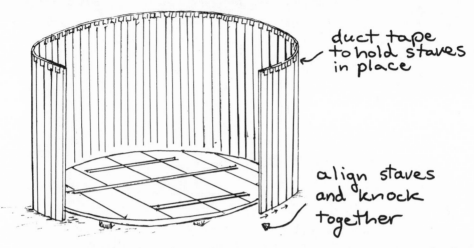

duct tape to hold staves in place

align staves and knock together

Illus. 37. After you have pounded the first two staves in, go back and pound the original stave as far as you can into the floor. Do this with the second stave, and in this manner, work your way around the tub. Secure the tops of the staves against one another with duct or electrical tape to keep them from shifting while you work.

Now, with all of the staves in place except for the last one, you will have to stop and pay some special attention to that final piece. No matter how precisely you think you may have measured, that last stave will not fit. It never has and it never will! Placement of the final stave is the job that separates the cooper men from the cooper boys. A skilled cooper will amaze and inhibit you with his or her ability to take a few quick measurements, rip the final stave, and simply pound it into place. The process, however, is not as simple as it looks.

First, you will have to determine the exact width for the final stave, measuring at the base of the tub (see Illus. 38). The width will probably be smaller than the original width you figured, so you will have to rip the stave lengthwise. Now, you must determine the final angle, which will probably vary from the original 4¼-degree angle at which you cut your other staves. To find this angle, measure the stave at the bottom—finding the inside length as well as the outside length. The inside is shorter than the outside, and forms a trapezoidal figure (see Illus. 39). Use a full-size construc-

49

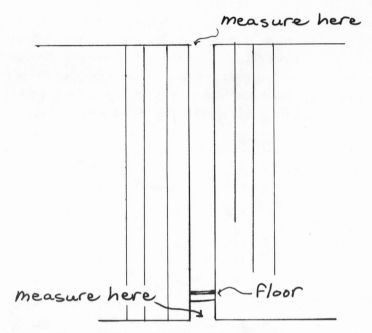

Illus. 38. To determine the exact width for the final stave, measure the gap at the base of the tub. The width will probably be smaller than what you had originally figured, so you will have to rip the stave lengthwise. To determine the angle of this stave, measure the stave at the bottom, finding the inside, as well as the outside, length.

tion diagram to draw your trapezoid to exact specifications. Now, take a protractor and measure your angles, set your table saw accordingly, and rip your final stave. If you have been perfectly accurate with your measurements, the stave should fit beautifully. If you have problems with this final stave, however, call in a friend or a professional with some coopering experience to help you out. The final stave has been known to stop many potential coopers right in their tracks, so don't be discouraged if you have to spend a little extra time and effort getting it right.

Illus. 39. The inside length of the stave is shorter than the outside length, and forms a trapezoidal figure.

With the last stave in position, you have completed the wall of your tub. It is now time to position your hoops.

The Hoops

The hoops can be made from a variety of metals. Some people have been known to use the steel band which lumber companies use to tie off wood and crated materials, but these are not very solid, and they have extremely sharp edges. The best hoops are made from either flexible steel or rounded wrought iron, and will provide your tub with lasting security. You want hoops that will be strong and durable, since there will be an extreme amount of pressure against the staves from the water and dislocation of that water inside the tub.

To hoop a tub 4 feet (1.22 m) in height, you will need four hoops. Each hoop should be 20 feet (6.10 m) in length, and ⅜-inch (9.53-mm) thick. They should be threaded on both ends. You will also need four lugs which you will use to join the hoops together and tighten them around the tub. Place the first hoop at the bottom of the tub, 4 inches (10.16 cm) from the base, so that it will help to secure the floorboards directly. It is recommended that you put your first hoop in this position since the base of the tub will require greater support than the top. Much of the weight and pressure of the water, not to mention the added human weight, will concentrate at the bottom of the tub. So, by securing your floor with this arrangement, you are concentrating support where it is needed most.

The easiest way to position your first hoop properly is to tack in a few nails around the tub, 4 inches (10.16 cm) from the base (see Illus. 40).

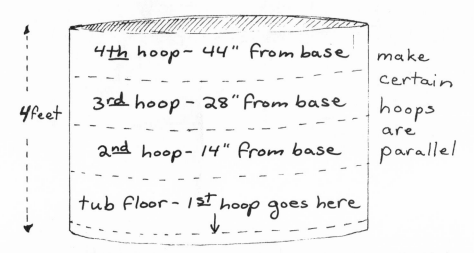

Illus. 40. Place the first hoop approximately 4 inches (10.16 cm) from the base of the tub, since the base requires greater support than the top. Place the second hoop 14 inches (35 cm) from the base, the third hoop 28 inches (70 cm) from the base, and the fourth hoop 44 inches (110 cm) from the base.

The hoop will rest on these nails. Now, take your hoop and bend it around the tub, allowing it to rest on the nails. Bring both ends through the lug, making sure that the ends span at least two staves (see Illus. 41). Stagger the lugs so they are not positioned one above another. Attach the washers and nuts and take up all of the slack. Do not tighten the hoop at this point— you will do that after all four hoops are in place so that the tension from them will be evenly distributed.

Place the second hoop 14 inches (35.56 cm) from the base. This will give you a 10-inch (25.4-cm) gap between the first and the second hoop, once again providing strength where strength is needed, close to the bottom. You can place the third hoop 28 inches (71.22 cm) from the base, and the fourth hoop 44 inches (111.76 cm) from the base. As you place each hoop in position, take up the slack but do not tighten.

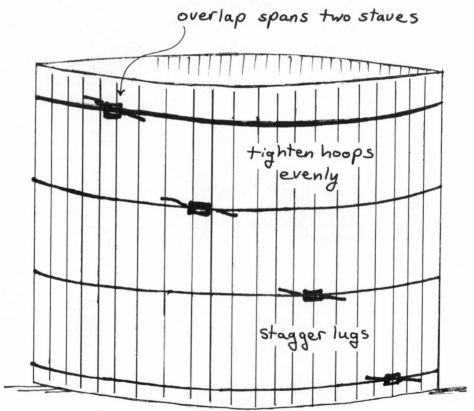

Illus. 41. Bring both ends of each hoop through a lug, making sure the ends span at least two staves. Stagger the lugs so they are not one above the other. Attach the washers and nuts and take up all slack. After all four hoops are in place, begin tightening them, starting with the bottom hoop. Then move to the second, third, and fourth hoops. Go back and repeat the process until the hoops are secure.

Now, you are ready to tighten the hoops, starting with the bottom hoop. At this time, it would be advisable to grab a friend and place him or her inside the tub with a rubber mallet or a piece of wood and a sledgehammer. (The wood placed between the sledge and the stave prevents any damage to the stave during pounding.) Now, begin tightening the hoops. As you tighten them, your friend inside the tub should watch the staves and pound those which may move or shift back into position. Once the bottom hoop is tightened, you can pound directly on the hoop. This will drive the staves even father into the floorboard and help to seat them securely.

With the bottom hoop tightened and secured, move to the second hoop and use the same procedure as with the first; then move to the third and fourth hoops. You will probably have some amount of flexing of the staves once you have tightened all four hoops, so go back to the beginning and repeat the process. Keep doing this until the hoops are absolutely secure, and the staves are evenly settled. At this time, do not forget to remove the nails which you have used as braces for the hoops.

Your basic tub is now finished. You will probably want to add some finishing touches to the main body at this time, like sanding down the top rim so that your guests do not get splinters while entering it. You also might want to round off the edges of the top rim, to make the tub even more comfortable.

Illus. 42. A rim decking around the tub will prevent splinters and make lounging about much more comfortable for you and your guests.

Your next major step will be to add the plumbing, that is, to secure the fixtures for drainage, filters, and jets. Prior to that, however, you should think about adding interior seats and a ladder. Even if you have extensive plans for adding decking around the tub, it would be more fun if you put the tub in working order as soon as possible. That way, after hard hours working on the decks, you will be able to soothe your muscles with a long, leisurely soak. Also, by adding the seats at this time, you will be able to determine where to place your hydrojets so that you will be taking the best advantage of the hot, swirling waters.

The Benches

Before installing the benches, decide where you want to place them, and at what height you want them. The best way to determine this is to get into your tub and crouch in a sitting position. Imagine the water level and adjust the bench height so that the water comes up to a point just beneath the shoulders. If you happen to stand 7 feet (2.13 m) tall, consider your friends' heights as well. Also, if small children are going to be using the tub, consider making a second seat at a higher level so they will not disappear under water when they sit down.

The perfect width for a bench is 8 inches (20.32 cm). Lay a 2 × 8 board across the tub and, on the underside, scribe along the wall of the tub and onto the wood (see Illus. 43). Then, saw off the excess wood along the curve you have just scribed. You can vary the length of your seat by moving the wood closer to the center of the tub or farther away. A hot tub that is 6 feet (1.83 m) in diameter will hold two good-sized benches facing one another.

For the ledgers which will support the seats, cut off 1-inch- (25-mm-) wide pieces from the excess wood you trimmed off your bench board. The angles are already there, where you had scribed along the tub wall, so you will be able to install the ledgers easily. Use 1½-inch (3.81-cm) screws and fasten the ledgers to the inside wall of the tub.

Prior to fastening your seats to the ledgers, it would be a good idea to do a thorough sanding job. You will want the seats to be as smooth and comfortable as possible, with the edges slightly rounded. When that is done, secure the seats to the ledgers, using 1-inch (25-mm) screws. Make certain that you countersink the screws, then sand the surface around the screw to make it as smooth as the rest of the seat. Of course, the positioning of the seats is entirely up to you. You may want to have a bench running

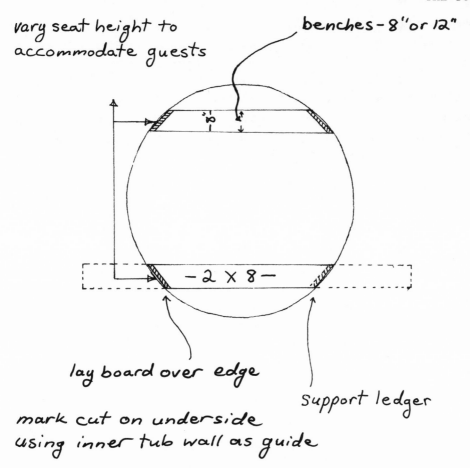

vary seat height to accommodate guests

benches - 8" or 12"

lay board over edge

support ledger

mark cut on underside using inner tub wall as guide

Illus. 43. To make benches, lay a 2 x 8 board across the tub and, using the inner tub wall as a guide, scribe the curve onto the underside of the wood. Eight inches (20.32 cm) is a perfect width for a bench. Install ledgers to support the bench, varying the height of the benches to accommodate guests' heights.

around the entire tub, or you may desire a series of step seats to accommodate as many varying heights of friends as possible. The important thing to remember is that the seats must be smooth, comfortable, and at a good height.

Since your tub is 4 feet (1.22 m) tall, plus another few inches (centimeters) with the foundation, you will probably want to build a ladder. The sides of the wooden steps should be 2 x 6 redwood, and angled off to a comfortable level. The steps should be about 18 inches (45.72 cm) across, and approximately 12 inches (30.48 cm) apart. Your top step, the one leading into the tub, should conform to the curve of the tub. Use the saber saw to cut this curve. Once again, since bare hands and feet will be using the steps, sand each piece to make certain that it is smooth. Round off as many sharp edges as possible. The last thing you want is your friends removing splinters from their hands while they're trying to enjoy your new hot tub.

If you plan to install a deck around your tub, or build next to a raised patio, you will not need steps. However, the steps are so easy and fast to construct that it would be worthwhile to make them so that you can use your tub while you're continuing to work around it.

The actual construction stage of your hot tub is now complete. If your drainage system is completed, you could, at this time, fill the tub. Normally, a new tub will spring a thousand leaks. As the redwood absorbs the water and expands, however, those leaks will disappear. It is a good idea to get the expansion stage over with as soon as possible, since it takes a few days for the tub to settle and secure itself. If the leaking does not stop, call a professional carpenter or lumberman and discuss methods of using mastic or some other waterproof substance to fill any existing gaps.

If all is well, however, your tub will be tight and secure within a matter of days. Now, you will begin adding the plumbing for your filter, heater, pump, and hydrojets.

The Plumbing System

Hot-tub purists will not go to extremes when installing plumbing for their tubs. A simple heating device and a pump usually suffice for their needs. Purists will not want a filter, since draining and cleaning their tubs is part of their hot-tubbing ritual. For most of us, however, a complete system that maintains hot, clean water, and incorporates the best in hydrojet fun is what we are after.

A simple system that costs a surprisingly small amount of money includes a heater, filter, water pump, and hydrojets (see Illus. 44-54). This system will keep the water clean and fresh, while also keeping the tub itself relatively clean. It will heat your water rapidly and the hydrojets will supply you with the bubbling waters that make hot tubbing so enjoyable.

California Cooperage

Illus. 44. The basic system of pump, filter, heater, and hydrojets is inexpensive and easy to install.

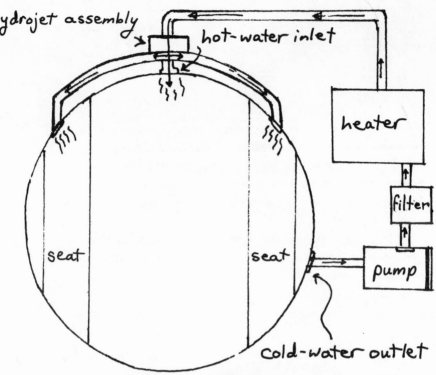

hydrojet assembly

hot-water inlet

heater

filter

pump

seat   seat

cold-water outlet

Illus. 45. A simple support system will keep the water clean, hot, and enjoyably bubbly. This diagram shows where to place each piece of equipment to best advantage.

The Floor Drain

Earlier on, I recommended that you drill the hole for the floor drain immediately after you had completed assembling the floor. Otherwise, if you wait until the tub is completed, you will have to turn it onto its side in order to cut the hole in the floor.

The floor drain should be a standard 2 5/16-inch (57.94-m) hole, since most fixtures are sized to fit this measurement. The drainage hole should be placed off to one side of the floor, about a half a foot (15.24 cm) from the side of the tub. A saw made specifically for the purpose of drilling holes should be used for all jobs on your tub. Used properly, this saw will prevent splintering and shattering of the floorboards and the staves when the time comes to drill your intake and outlet holes on the side of the tub. Talk to your local carpenter and ask him about the saw—he can suggest one that will make your job easy and successful.

Once you have drilled the hole, you can then install the drain. When using threaded plumbing fixtures in all phases of assembly with regards to your hot tub, always wrap Teflon[TM] around the threads and apply some PVC

60

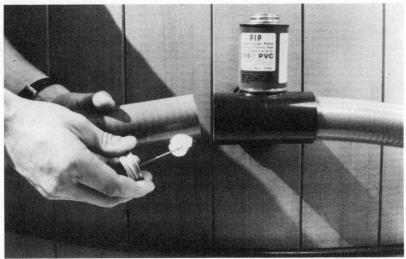

California Cooperage

(Above) Illus. 46. When using threaded plumbing fixtures, always wrap Teflon around the threads and apply some PVC weld to the threads. This will guarantee a secure fit and will also waterproof the linkage. (Below) Illus. 47. This tub cutaway shows the jets, suction, recessed floor drain, seat, and general tub construction.

California Cooperage

weld to the threads. This will guarantee a secure fit and will also waterproof the linkage. When you purchase your pipes and fittings from your local plumbing outlet, you can get a good recommendation for the best products to use.

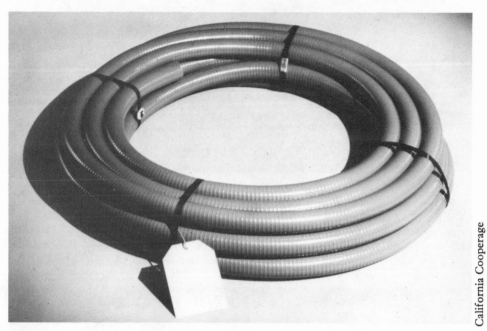

California Cooperage

Illus. 48. When you purchase your pipes and plumbing fittings, get a professional's recommendation for the best products to use. Pictured here is California Cooperage's flexible PVC hose.

Install the drain simply by placing the nut on the underside of the floor, and lining it up with the hole. Take the drain itself and screw it down through the hole, until the outer rim is flush with the floor. Tighten the nut by hand, then use a wrench to secure it. Do not tighten the nut to the point where it destroys the threads or bites into the wood. The Teflon and the weld will serve to seal off your joint and waterproof it perfectly. Now, take a piece of plastic pipe, a PVC elbow, and a hose bib, and secure them to the drain. Make certain that your hose bib extends beyond the edge of the tub. This makes it easier to attach the hose when you want to drain the tub.

The Inlet and Outlet

You will need to drill two more holes on the sides of your tub for the inlet and outlet systems. These holes are needed where water is pulled from your tub, looped through the pump, filter, and heater and then returned

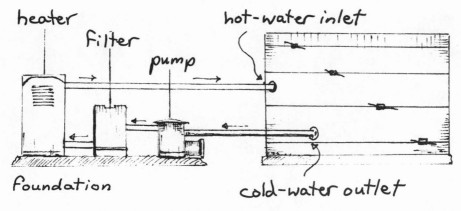

heater

filter

pump

hot-water inlet

Foundation

cold-water outlet

Illus. 49. The inlet hole in the tub carries water from the heater and should be positioned as close to the heater as possible. The outlet hole carries water from the tub into the pump, and so should be as near to the pump as possible.

via the inlet. The outlet hole should be drilled near the base of the tub, approximately 8 inches (20.32 cm) from the floor. The pipe will carry this water directly into the pump, so drill the hole as close as possible to where your pump will be. The inlet hole will carry water directly from the heater, so the position here should be as close to the heater as possible. The inlet hole should be approximately 30 inches (76.20 cm) above the floor. Both holes should be 2 5/16 inches (57.94 mm) in diameter .

Hydrojets

Decide where you want to place your hydrojets, and drill two 2 5/16-inch (57.94 mm) holes. Placement of the hydrojets is a matter of personal taste, but most people prefer them from 6 inches (15.24 cm) to a foot and a half (45.72 mm) above the seats. Many bathers love the feel of the jets directly against their tired muscles, and use the force of the hot-water jets as a soothing massage. A hydrojet assembly kit can be purchased from a local hot-tub dealer, or a retail outlet selling pool equipment. You will find directions with the kit for installation of the hydrojet system.

Illus. 50. Close-up of the hydrojet fitting. The invigorating force of the hot water jets acts as a soothing massage against tired muscles.

California Cooperage

63

California Cooperage

Illus. 51. Cutaway view of California Cooperage's hydrojet fitting.

Now that you have drilled the holes, you should determine where you will be placing your units. It is advisable to place your pump, filter, and heater on concrete, and in a place where they will not affect the bather's entry into the tub. The sequence in which you set up your units always remains the same. Water from the tub will be sucked out through the outlet into the pump, then it will move through the filter and into the heater. From there, it returns to the tub via the inlet. The placement of the filter between the pump and the heater insures that the water entering the heater will be free of particles that could clog or harm the piping inside the heater itself. You should use 1⅜-inch (34.53-mm) piping. From the tub to the pump, you should use rubber fuel line—the type used in washing machines is acceptable. The piping between the pump and the filter and heater can be the same diameter, but it should be made of copper. You can also use rubber fuel line from the heater into the inlet and hydrojet assembly. How you construct and design the piping system between the units is entirely up to you. Some people prefer to hide the pipes by burying them, or constructing a simple wood shed around them so they won't detract from the ambience of the tub itself.

One suggestion when laying your pipes is to place a turn-off valve between the pump and the tub. This will allow you to stop the water flow when you want to clean or repair your tub.

The Heater

You have a choice as to the kind of heater you will be using for your tub. You can select from gas, electric, or solar (see page 71). You may want to save money and pick up an old household water heater from a junkyard, or you may want a more efficient model that heats quickly and efficiently. If you choose to heat with either gas or electricity, then you should go with a gas heater. Even with today's rising prices, gas is still cheaper than electricity, and there are plenty of options available to you when choosing a gas heater.

California Cooperage

Illus. 52. This natural gas heater is only one of the options available to you when choosing a gas heater. Or, check into an electric or solar-heating system.

First, there is the aforementioned household water heater. The drawbacks of these heaters should be compared to the advantage of their low-cost availability. They are very slow, and in some cases will take nearly half a day to raise the temperature of your tub to 104° F. (40° C.). They are also quite large and unsightly. But, the fact remains that they are easy to find and are often available for free.

Another type of heater is the old-fashioned cast-iron model with the coiled copper tubing which is heated by a burner. This type is much more efficient than the water heater, taking approximately half the time to heat your tub. It is also available from junkyards for a nominal fee.

One of the more efficient heaters is the large flash heater that is capable of heating a thousand gallons of water 25 degrees in one hour. The flash heater is not aesthetically appealing in that it makes an inordinate amount of noise, but it is strikingly efficient.

Probably the best buy in heaters is the simple pool heater. Used or new, it is extremely efficient and costs only pennies a day to run. Built to heat thousands of gallons of water, these heaters will do the job quickly and efficiently. They are relatively small, and do not make a lot of noise. A good pool heater can get your tub water ready in less than half an hour.

California Cooperage

Illus. 53. Cutaway view of the pump and filter unit. A good filter will elimi-nate impurities and keep the water in your tub fresh and clean.

New pool heaters are available at any pool supply store. Used pool heaters can be found in abundance wherever swimming pools are sold, and you can purchase one for less than $100. Most hot-tub enthusiasts highly recommend the pool heater. They love its ability to heat the tub quickly, thus allowing for spontaneous bathing. Purists will ritualize every aspect of hot-tub bathing, and that includes waiting around for the tub to get hot. Most people, however, do not have a lot of time to spend preparing their tubs for a soak. The majority of hot tubbers think a flick of the switch and a half-hour wait is time enough !

Remember when purchasing your heater that you have approximately 1,000 gallons of water to heat to a temperature of 105° F. (406° C.). The heating capacity of your equipment will be measured in terms of BTU's —British thermal units. A BTU simply means the amount of heat required to raise one pound of water one degree. Your dealer will provide you with a BTU chart, showing you exactly how efficient his heaters are in terms of the time it takes his equipment to heat the water. Since pool heaters are designed to heat thousands of gallons of water quickly, they should be perfect for use in a hot tub.

After you have heated your tub and you and your friends are enjoying your soak, keep the heater on simmer. Heat loss occurs in a tub because of contact with the air, the absorption of heat by the people in the tub, and the loss of heat due to the hydrojet system. An efficient solution for heat loss is to include a thermostat so that your water will be maintained at a constant temperature throughout the soak.

The Filter

Your hot tub is, in fact, a miniature swimming pool. Most people would find it inconceivable not to filter the water in their swimming pools, and the same holds true with people who own hot tubs. Without a filter, constant draining and cleansing of the tub will be necessary, and only the purists are willing to accept those terms. A good filter will eliminate impurities and keep the water in your tub fresh and clean.

The filter system used in most swimming pools is the diatomaceous earth system. It is simple, inexpensive, and as effective as they come. The filter is a simple piece of equipment consisting of stainless steel housing and a filter pad that is made up of microscopic green algae. The system also includes a gauge that continually monitors the pressure. Ask your dealer about the acceptable pressures for your particular tub. These will vary according to the size of your tub. The addition of the filter system will make your hot-tub experience even more enjoyable.

California Cooperage

Illus. 54. The 12 kW electric spa heater and filter pump shown here is a highly efficient system, sold by California Cooperage, which will quickly heat and circulate clean water in your tub.

The Pump

The pump is used to circulate the water through the filter, through the heater, and into the tub. A simple water pump is all that you will need for this purpose. The horsepower of your pump will depend on whether or not you are using hydrojets.

The basic formula for a pump is that one horsepower will circulate 80 gallons of water per minute. For a 1,000-gallon tub, you are then looking at a cycle of slightly less than thirteen minutes. If you have hydrojets, you should add ½ horsepower for each jet. The pump supplies the power to activate those jets. So, for a 1,000-gallon tub with two hydrojets, you should be installing a 2-horsepower pump.

When positioning your pump, keep it low to the ground so that it will retain its prime. Also, install a casing around it to keep leaves and other objects out. The water from the tub will be going directly into the pump, so it's a good idea to place a copper screen in the tub outlet to prevent large particles from leaving the tub and entering the pump. One other note about using the pump: Make certain that it is turned on prior to turning on your heater. This will prevent the steam from gathering, and eventually from blowing out, the pump.

Illus. 55. Stretch out for a peaceful time by yourself with a leisurely, re-laxing soak.

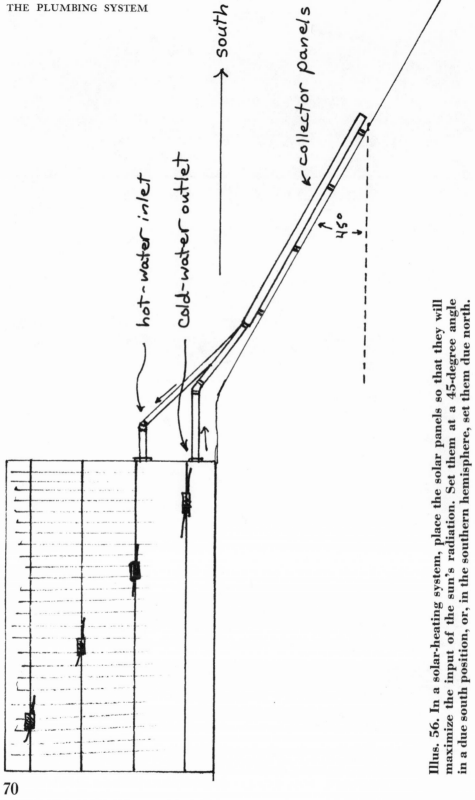

Illus. 56. In a solar-heating system, place the solar panels so that they will maximize the input of the sun's radiation. Set them at a 45-degree angle in a due south position, or, in the southern hemisphere, set them due north.

The System

You can save money by purchasing your heater, filter, and pump secondhand and by doing your own plumbing. However, there are problems with used equipment that you should be careful to avoid. Used equipment can be faulty, and if you are not particularly adept at repairing pumps and heaters, you might want to consider the alternative. Hot-tub dealers will sell you the entire system—this includes heater, pump, filter, hydrojet assembly, and all preassembled plumbing. Check out these systems and compare prices, taking into consideration the guarantee offered and how easy installation will be.

Solar Heating

Solar heating has already become a reasonable alternative to gas and electric heating. In the past decade, solar technology has developed to the point where heating from the sun's radiation has become a viable economic investment for the average homeowner. Because of the energy crisis and the escalating costs of fossil fuels, many state governments have offered tax credits to homeowners who elect to go solar, making the investment even more appealing. The *most* appealing quality of solar heating is that once you have installed your system, your fuel bills will decrease dramatically. The sun will provide you with much of the energy you need, and the repairs of a solar-heating system are virtually nonexistent.

The solar-heating system is quite simple. It consists of collector panels supported by a steel casing. The panels are constructed of etched glass which serves to trap the sun's heat without releasing it. Beneath the glass are aluminum fins through which copper tubing runs. The aluminum conducts the heat from the glass to the copper tubing, thus heating the water that passes through the tubing. Depending upon the size of the panel and the part of the country in which you live, a solar-heating system can work just as efficiently as a gas heater.

The location of your panels is of extreme importance when considering a solar-heating system. Your first consideration should be to place your panels so that they will maximize the input of the sun's radiation. For a stable system, simply use a compass and set your panels in a due-south position (see Illus. 56). In the southern hemisphere, you would want to set them due north. Then, set your panels at a 45-degree angle. This will maximize the sun's input into your panels throughout the year. You can also construct a hinged frame for your panels so that you can alter the angle according to the seasons, increasing it during the winter months when the sun is

American Solar Energy Systems

Illus. 57. The glass collector panels used in a solar-heating system trap the sun's heat without releasing it. Beneath the glass are aluminum fins through which copper tubing runs. The aluminum conducts the heat from the glass to the copper tubing, thus heating the water that passes through the tubing.

lower on the horizon, and decreasing it in the summer when the sun is directly overhead.

Once you have decided on and calculated the best position for your panels, keep in mind that the shade of a nearby tree or house is undesirable. Also, consider placing your solar heater at least a foot (30.48 cm) beneath the bottom level of your tub. The reason for this is something called "thermal siphon," a principle involving the actions of hot versus cold water. In your tub, the cold water will naturally sink to the bottom, while the hot water will rise to the surface. If your solar heater is beneath the level of the tub, the cold water will flow from its outlet by force of gravity and into your solar heater. Once there, the heated water will move uphill and back into the tub through the hot-water inlet. Setting your solar heater in such a position as to maximize the flow of water through the thermal siphon principle could eliminate the need for a pump. If you do, drill your holes for the cold-water outlet about 8 inches (20.32 cm) from the bottom of the tub. The hole for the inlet should be 2 feet (60.96 cm) or so from the bottom. When you purchase your solar panels, ask your salesman about thermal siphon, and how to best plumb the solar-heating system to avoid air locks and back-ups.

If you decide to place your solar system above the bottom level of the tub, thus not taking advantage of the thermal-siphon process, then you will need a pump. You should also include the filter, no matter where you are locating the solar panels.

If you live in a temperate zone, like California or Florida, you will find that solar heaters work with undying efficiency. If an area like Minnesota is your home, you might want to consider adding a small gas-heater system to augment the work of the solar system. In that latitude, the amount of radiation penetrating the atmosphere is distinctly less, and will affect the proficiency of your system.

It would be a good idea to include within your solar-heating system a control mechanism whereby sensors for hot and cold water can regulate the temperature of your tub. Otherwise, a solar heater will continue working as long as you let it, and can raise the temperature of your tub to an uncomfortable level.

Today, there are hundreds of companies producing solar collectors and systems. It is best to shop around and compare products to find the

Redwood in the Round

Illus. 58. The naturally warm and humid atmosphere of this "greenhouse" setting enables indoor hot-tub bathing with all the openness and sunshine of an outdoor location.

right design for your tub. Professionals should be able to recommend the perfect system for your needs, and show you how best to capitalize on your area and location. Solar heat is inexpensive once the initial investment is made. It is ecologically sound, and will work for you over an extended period of time. And, if we face extreme fuel shortages in the future, you will be able to alleviate some of your friends' depression and worries by inviting them over for a naturally heated hot-tub soak. That, in itself, might be enough to recommend solar heating!

Accessories, Maintenance, and Amenities

Your tub is now functional. The foundation, the tub, and the heating and pumping systems are in place. However, there are a few other measures you should take to make certain that your tub stays in good condition.

First, it would be wise to build or buy a simple wooden cover for your tub. This should be a flat piece of insulated redwood large enough to cover the tub. The cover will keep out leaves and other debris, while helping to retain some of the heat from the tub after a soak. The tub will also heat faster with a lid on. You should keep your tub covered at all times

Illus. 59. The extensive decking, fencing, and roofing in this hot-tub environment offers a shaded, secluded soak with immediate access to the house.

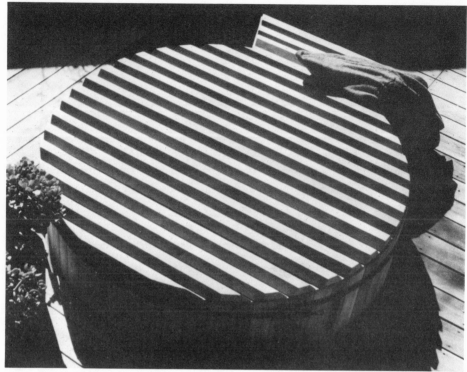

California Cooperage

(Above) Illus. 60. An insulated wooden cover for your tub will not only keep out leaves and other debris, but will also retain some of the heat in the tub after a soak, and will help the water to heat up faster.

(Below) Illus. 61. This California Cooperage insulated wood and foam roll-top cover can easily be rolled up by one person. Hardware secures the roll-top to a bracket located off the tub's edge, so the cover always stays in place, whether rolled up or flat.

California Cooperage

Illus. 62. To maintain crystal-clear, pure tub water, you should add chlorine at regular intervals, and clean the interior of the tub at least twice a year.

when it is not in use. Your filter, heater, and pump should also be protected from the elements. Small wooden sheds to protect the equipment will suffice.

You should treat the water in your tub in much the same way as you would treat swimming-pool water. That is, you should add chlorine at regular intervals to maintain purity. Most pool-supply houses carry a small kit which contains not only packets of chlorine and a recommendation for their use, but also acid-testing kits that will measure the pH level of your water. Talk to the salesman and find out which kit will work most efficiently for your tub size.

You should clean the interior of the tub at least once every six months. This means draining the tub, washing out the interior, and refilling it. At this time, you should also clean out the screens in the outlet pipes, in the filter, and in the pump system. A regular maintenance program will insure that your tub stays in top shape with minimal effort on your part.

California Cooperage

Illus. 63. Some of the extras—practical and otherwise—to make your tub even more enjoyable:

A. Bubbler system
B. Rim decking
C. Steps
D. Hand skimmer, to remove debris from the tub
E. Body towels
F. Filter cartridge replacements
G. Tub scents
H. A rubber ducky, of course!
I. Outdoor drenching shower.

The Hot-Tub Environment

THE OUTDOOR TUB

Most new owners of hot tubs have discovered that their tubs quickly become centers of activities in their yards. Because of this, most owners sooner or later want to add a total environment for their tub, one that includes decking, the proper lighting, and even a sound system.

Illus. 64. A basic tub, platform, and steps, plus a few plants and a couple of trees—and your outdoor tub is ready for use. It's also easily movable.

Decking and Drainage

Decking around your tub is always a good idea. It provides easy access to the tub, and a gathering place for those who are not soaking. If you decide to build decking, use the anchor bolts which you have set into your foundation as the base hinges upon which the deck will rest (see page 29). The decking should be made of good lumber, preferably redwood, and should be sanded and treated to remove splinters. Remember, too, that a deck should provide spacing for water drainage. Prior to laying out your deck, it might be a good idea to create a natural drainage ditch beneath it by excavating the ground on a slight angle, and even by laying down some aluminum to move the water. This will prevent water from gathering beneath your deck and eventually rotting out the wood.

Illus. 65. Decking around your tub provides easy access to the tub and a sitting area for after-soaking sunbathing.

Benches and Platforms

When building the deck, consider adding benches and platforms for your guests to rest on after a soak. A wall section with pegs for hanging clothes and towels would also provide a nice touch. The best way to plan your environment here is to think in terms not only of the soak, but of those moments before and after. Make your tub a center of social activities and you will find that its presence adds dramatically to your pleasures.

Temperature Variations

One of the most exhilarating experiences of hot tubbing is soaking in a tub and then jumping into a cold-water pool. This practice is widespread, and people with strong constitutions swear by it. If you do not have a swimming pool near your tub, you might want to install a showerhead or even a hose attachment near the tub so that your friends can enjoy the rush of cold water immediately upon leaving the tub. In warm weather, the cold-water soaking will cool everyone off in a delightful manner. On cold nights, you will probably find that merely leaving the tub provides enough of a contrast in temperature to effect the same reaction.

Illus. 66. After a long, hot soak in a bubbling hot tub like this, some hardy spirits like to jump into a cold-water pool. For less adventuresome souls, merely leaving the tub and stepping out into the cool air provides enough of a contrast in temperature.

85

Lighting

Lighting around the hot tub can provide you with a delightful environment. Most people prefer soft lighting, the kind that bathes the area around it in indirect, soothing hues. You can simply use the standard outdoor floodlights for this effect, bouncing the beams off a tree, or placing them on the ground and shooting the beam up against the tub. Or, a simple string of Christmas lights can provide a beautiful glow around your tub. When setting up the lighting, keep in mind that some people are quite inhibited about their bodies, and that the softer the lighting, the more comfortable your guests will be. Also, remember to string your electrical cords in such a fashion as to prevent them from becoming wet. Protect all connections and sockets with electrical tape. Lighting fixtures designed for outdoor use should fulfill these needs well.

Music

Most people love music, and soft music around a hot tub adds tremendously to the enjoyment of a soak. A couple of speakers, suspended from a tree and hooked up to your stereo system inside the house, will suffice to create a beautiful audio environment for your soaks.

Other Touches

There are hundreds of other touches which you might consider for your tub that will make it a social hub. Incense around the tub will dispel the smell of chlorine. A collection of nice warm towels for your friends on a cold night will be appreciated. If you serve liquid refreshments, always use paper or plastic cups. Broken glass in the bottom of a tub is almost impossible to locate.

The environment for your outdoor tub will change as you use it more and more. Soon, you will begin to develop a style all your own, one that reflects your personality and the manner in which you enjoy entertaining. You will find yourself constantly adding and altering the area around your tub, experimenting with it until you get it just perfect.

California Cooperage

Illus. 67. A tranquil, relaxing hot-water massage can be a most enjoyable break from your daily routine. Be sure to avoid extremes—keep temperatures at a safe level (see page 95) and limit your soak to about half an hour.

Illus. 68 and 69. Plants, brick, rock, wood, and plenty of light create a natural environment around an indoor tub. Pay attention to special requirements for indoor installation, page 89.

Redwood in the Round

Redwood in the Round

88

THE INDOOR TUB

If you decide to place your tub indoors, you should concern yourself with a few necessities of indoor bathing.

First, your heating, filtering, and pumping units should be placed against the wall, with an exhaust outlet. This will prevent gas fumes and other unpleasantries from invading the air around the hot tub. The noise level of these units will also be increased indoors, so think about insulating them to keep the sound down.

Second, the walls of the room in which you have located your tub should be made of a wood panelling. The panels will insulate the room while absorbing the moisture from the tub itself.

Third, the placement of windows should be such that good air circulation is possible. Nearly everyone has suffered the discomfort of swimming indoors where there is poor air circulation. The steam from the pool fills the air, along with noxious fumes from the chlorine. A fresh-air intake duct, say from a central air conditioning system, combined with adjustable windows on opposite walls, will allow you to regulate the flow of fresh air throughout the room.

In conjunction with the windows, you might want to consider adding a skylight directly above your tub. The skylight will provide sunlight, and will allow the escape of heat and steam from the tub. You will also want an exhaust vent on the wall directly above your support system to channel out any fumes missed by the direct exhaust system.

Fourth, the decking should be made of wood, spaced to provide for proper drainage. The floor should be sloped towards the drain, and the drain itself should be hooked up to your sewage pipe running beneath the floor.

The foundation of the interior tub should be made of concrete, and as strong as that of the outdoor tub.

Essentially, then, the indoor tub requires special considerations to prevent the room in which your tub is sitting from becoming a steam bath. With proper thought to air circulation and heat control, you can create an indoor environment totally suitable for hot tubbing—one that will function beautifully in all climates. So, if you live in a cold, northern climate and do not possess the rugged constitution that allows for jumping into the snow after a hot-tub soak, you might give serious thought to locating your tub indoors.

*   *   *

Your hot-tub environment will undoubtedly become an integral part of the success of your tub. How you design that environment depends on personal taste, the location of your land, and the use you will make of your tub. As mentioned in an earlier section of this book, it is wise to think through all aspects of your tub prior to the construction and laying of the foundation. A general, overall plan for your yard and the area surrounding the tub, even if not implemented immediately, will allow you the option to build later on. Give thought to every aspect of the hot-tub experience, and common sense, as well as taste, will dictate your design for the environment.

California Cooperage

Illus. 70. The environment you design for your tub is a matter of personal taste and the location of your land. Give plenty of thought to an overall plan for your yard before you begin construction.

The Social and Health
Aspects of
Hot Tubbing

HOT WATER AND HEALTH

Throughout the ages, human beings have sought hot water as a remedy for what ailed them. For some, the search led to exotic mountain springs where natural mineral waters erupted hot and sulfuric from the bowels of the earth. Others simply tried their hand at constructing their own baths by igniting huge fires beneath stone tubs. No matter how extensive their search for a hot soak, however, all had in common the certainty that hot-water soaking was good for them. They were not misled.

In the 4th century B.C., Hippocrates, the father of medicine, recommended hot-water bathing as a means of curing illness, and the stampede began. People suffering from a wide variety of ailments searched the countryside for natural hot springs, believing not only that water itself provided a cure, but that the ingredients of that water (minerals and natural chemicals) were also beneficial. These early enthusiasts were correct in their assumptions, although scientific knowledge at the time was not able to explain exactly why hot-mineral baths were successful in curing some forms of illness.

The curative qualities of water were widely accepted in Western civilization by the time the 19th century rolled around and the father of hydrotherapy, a Prussian named Vincenz Priessnitz, arrived on the scene. Priessnitz made himself a fine living by promoting the idea that massage through water and a disciplined program of bathing could result in amazing cures for diseases and illnesses. Priessnitz experimented with hoses and hand pumps to circulate water in tubs, charging his royal patients exorbitant fees for the privilege of undergoing his cure. The good doctor was obviously something of a scam artist, but in fact, he did have the right idea and people throughout Europe seemed to love his methods.

Water therapy literally arrived with Priessnitz, and in the century following his success, hydrotherapy has developed into a science. Hydrotherapy is used extensively to help rehabilitate people suffering from crippling diseases, to provide therapy for those who have become crippled as a result of an accident or wound, and to help those suffering from psychological problems. In America today, there are hundreds of retreats that rely on water therapy as the foundation for their success. One of these is Esalen, a popular retreat located on a bluff overlooking the Pacific Ocean in California's Big Sur country. Esalen became quite popular during the 1960's when new mental and physical disciplines were popular. People who went there seeking a respite from the schizoid 20th century found that hydrotherapy offered a soothing relief to modern-day stress.

Retreats such as Esalen in the United States, Baden-Baden in Germany, and Vichy in France were widely heralded as health centers. Those who regularly attended these retreats believed that they had succeeded not only in curing themselves, but in increasing their longevity. The only problem with the world-famous retreats was the cost—the average man or woman was prohibited from enjoying the benefits of the baths simply because he or she could not afford them. It seemed, once again, that staying

Illus. 71. The wine-vat origins of the California hot tub are evident in the simple design of this tub. The basic idea and fun of splashing around in an "overgrown pail" of water remain the same.

healthy and living to a ripe old age was a luxury reserved only for the wealthy. However, the pioneer spirit of the California subculture once again succeeded in cutting through all the upper-class red tape when some people from Santa Barbara took an old wine vat and transformed it into a hot tub. The luxury of hot-water bathing, plus its medical and emotional benefits, were finally available to the common man.

Essentially, the three elements that contribute to the effectiveness of hot-water bathing are the hot water, the massage created by the pressure of hydrojets, and the minerals. Healthwise, the only elements missing from the hot-tub cure are the minerals. Although most experts say that the mineral content of natural hot springs is beneficial, they also remind those who are without access to natural hot springs that those very same minerals are easily introduced into the body through means such as vitamin pills. So, the hot tub with its hot waters and massage jets provides a naturally healthful bathing experience, one that is accessible to almost everyone.

The temperature of the water in a hot tub is normally around 105°F. (40.6°C.). In some countries, such as Japan, hot-water bathing is more akin to bathing in scalding water, with temperatures set as high as 120°F. (48.8°C.). One is cautioned against such extremes, since the temperature endurance level for the human body is right around that figure. If you have ever attempted to step into a tub that is 120°F. (48.8°C.), no more needs to be said. There is quite a difference between an enjoyable hot-tub soak and self-immolation by water! Stick with 105°F. (40.6°C.) and you will not only enjoy yourself, but you will also survive to enjoy the health benefits.

At 105°F. (40.6°C.), the water will perform a number of beneficial functions. It will cause the muscles to relax, thus releasing tension on the fiber and untying those muscular knots that can plague you. The hydrojets of the hot tub will also work the muscles and relax them in the same beneficial way as a massage, and it will probably be a lot more fun. Hot water will cause the blood vessels to dilate, which is beneficial in that the circulation will be increased and strengthened. You will also find that during a soak, the pores of the skin will dilate, and when leaving the tub and coming in contact with cool air, or the cool water of a shower or pool, those pores will snap shut. This is excellent therapy for "tired" skin.

Physicians agree that soaking in a hot tub is good for people with heart trouble and high blood pressure. However, anyone who has suffered a stroke or is suffering from hardening of the arteries should consult a physician prior to soaking in a hot tub.

The cosmetic benefits of a hot-tub soak are numerous, and there are thousands of healthy men and women who are living proof that hot tubbing does wonders for the complexion. The cleansing of the pores and the beneficial effects upon the circulation of the blood, as described above, tend to result in healthy, clean-glowing skin. Hot tubbing, in moderation, simply tends to make people look better. One note about the skin and the respiratory system with regard to soaking: Remember that you are sitting in swirling waters with a temperature of 105°F. (40.6°C.). Overdoing it can result in some uncomfortable reactions to the skin and to your system. Use the tub wisely. Begin soaking in short intervals and gradually build up your time to a point where you feel comfortable. The average soak usually lasts about half an hour.

There is no doubt that, for most people, hot tubbing is healthful, invigorating, and fun. It is an excellent way to tone the skin, help the circulation, and rid yourself of muscular problems.

THE SOCIAL SCENE

It is often said that California leads the rest of the nation in introducing fads and trends, and hot tubbing is definitely a California phenomenon. It began in California, and the social rituals that have evolved around hot tubbing are strictly Californian in nature. Of course, there are no laws requiring you to follow a certain routine prior to and during a hot-tub soak, but you will enjoy your hot-tub experience more if you acknowledge and understand certain social amenities.

Clothed vs. Nude Bathing

There are a great many people, especially in that vanguard state of California, who profess that hot tubbing in any kind of clothing whatsoever is tantamount to committing a mortal sin. Group nudity in California has always been fairly common, and many Californians think nothing of stripping down with friends and frolicking in water. Communal nude bathing is, of course, a matter of personal taste and choice, and one of the main considerations when making that choice revolves most naturally around sexual attitudes. The sight of a group of naked people sharing the small space of a hot tub, will raise many eyebrows. From outside the tub, one cannot imagine anything less than an orgy taking place. The fact is, however, that the effect of the hot water in a hot tub is to induce a complete state of relaxation that serves to dissolve sexual and other energies.

A phenomenon occurs when nude people bathe together in a tub. The sense of communal sharing and the closeness that results from a hot-tub soak, breaks down the barriers that isolate average human beings from one another in society. People soaking together in a tub tend to feel themselves isolated as a group from the rest of the world, and thus they begin to feel closer to one another. They share the common water and the common

California Cooperage

Illus. 72. How many friendly souls can you fit in a hot tub? Find out for yourself! Hot tubs are quickly becoming the social hub of the home entertainment scene.

experience. And, when bathing nude, they naturally open themselves up to one another in a more dramatic fashion than they normally would in their everyday lives. Hot tubbers tend to be very frank with one another, delving into areas that require trust and compassion on the part of the listener. This is one of the reasons that so many therapists and psychiatrists are using communal bathing as an effective environment for group therapy sessions. Hot water, honesty, and friendship seem to go hand in hand.

Sexual Conduct

Of course, there has to be some amount of sexuality involved when people gather together in the nude, but whatever a particular group of people does together has little bearing on the hot tub itself. Sex can or cannot be an integral part of the hot-tub experience. It all depends on the individuals and their preferences.

The social aspects of the hot tub revolve around the concept of pleasure. Your principal concerns will revolve around your guests' comfort. In other words, as a hot-tub host, you should consider whatever you can do to make the soak more pleasurable. Make sure there is easy access to the tub, and if you are soaking in the nude, keep the lighting low to help your shy friends out. Provide places to hang towels, and keep a few extra robes around for those who have forgotten to bring their own.

Refreshments

If you decide to serve refreshments, pour only the lightest of alcoholic beverages. The stimulus of the tub combined with the effect of strong alcohol can be uncomfortable as well as detrimental. The best refreshments to serve are light, cheery wines and beer. They just seem to go better naturally than, say, a Manhattan. And remember, serve your drinks in paper or plastic cups. Real glass around a tub can be disastrous!

Food

Food is not a particularly good idea during a soak. First, liquid refreshment is so much more satisfying. And second, you do not want crumbs floating around in your tub. You will discover that you do not want to eat heavily after a soak—a light snack of cheese and bread always works well. Heavy foods work counter to the light, restful feeling you will have.

Drugs

It is wise to avoid all drugs before and during a soak. Your pulse rate and respiratory system go through some fairly extreme changes when you immerse yourself in the 105°F. (40.6°C.) water. If you have taken stimulants or depressants into your system, the reaction is that much more severe. Most drugs do not mix well with any kind of physical exertion. Consider a soak in your tub the same as strenuous physical activity, and common sense will guide you.

Keep your hot tub clean, respectable, and inviting. Make it an expression of your own pleasure consciousness and you will succeed in drawing out all the potential of a hot-tub experience. Your hot tub will soon prove itself to be one of the finest investments you have ever made. Its dividends will come back to you in the forms of health, fun, and extremely pleasurable social interaction. And beyond that, you will find that after a late-night soak you will sleep better than you have in years.

Redwood in the Round

Illus. 73. A clean, inviting hot tub is the perfect meeting spot for a family get-together—to sit, talk, and enjoy each other's company.

Illus. 74. Indoors, wood panelling will insulate the room and absorb moisture from the tub. An overhead skylight will provide sunlight and allow the escape of heat and steam from the tub.

Redwood in the Round

Redwood in the Round

Illus. 75. Plumbing fixtures are kept well out of sight in this outdoor tub. Soft lighting and music will add that extra special touch, but remember to string electrical wires in such a way as to prevent them from getting wet.

100

Hot-Water Bathing
and Mankind

The popularity of hot-water bathing, privately or in groups, has had its ups and downs throughout the history of civilization. Not all cultures have stressed bodily cleanliness and the resurgence of the soul that results from a plunge into hot water. In fact, some early cultures left no traces of bathing facilities whatsoever.

The earliest records we have of baths were found among the remains of the Egyptian civilizations, predominantly in the ruins of palaces. These records indicate that the Egyptians erected separate structures for the purpose of bathing. However, archaeologists have been unable to resurrect these structures intact in order to formulate a complete picture of what bathing was like in that era.

The best early records of bathing we possess are found in the ruins of the early Aegean civilizations, dating back to 1700 B.C. These ruins show extremely sophisticated architectural design for bathrooms, with carefully planned plumbing facilities and extremely proficient designs for moving water from its source and into the bathroom itself.

The Greek civilization's ultimate rise to its zenith of thought and sophistication (5th century B.C.) also carried with it a rise in the popularity of bathing. In Athens, public bathhouses were popular among the wealthy. The facilities were very large, designed to provide the visitor with every possible bodily comfort. Exercise rooms, massage rooms, cold-water plunges, and conversational areas were located throughout these beautiful structures. There, men like Socrates and his student Plato spent many hours getting rubdowns with exotic oils, plunging into the cool waters, and discoursing on the development of Western thought. These great bathhouses were designed for the use of the elite, and remained off-limits to the common man of Greece.

The Romans carried on the Greek tradition of public bathhouses, and developed some innovations of their own. Their bathing structures were designed much like those of the Greeks, and the spirit of the houses was very much the same as that which prevailed within the Grecian spas. The Romans, however, revolutionized the art of bathing by making one vital addition. They provided three separate types of bathing for their guests—hot water, warm water, and cold water. At this time, hot-water pools were used mainly to create steam. The cool-water pools were used following the steam bath to lower the body temperature. The Roman citizen took his or her bath according to a set routine, which usually involved anointment of the body with oils, exercise, massages, and plunges into the pools. The bathhouses were incredibly elaborate buildings, housing everything from shops to gardens where the bather, after a stimulating session in the baths, could reflect on life. Records of Roman baths are best preserved within the ruins of Pompeii, which was levelled in 79 A.D. by the eruption of Mount Vesuvius. There, archaeologists have discovered the two oldest Roman public baths still in existence, both of which have two sets of bathrooms, one for men and one for women.

Illus. 76. Bath, a medicinal spa in England, flourished in the 18th and early 19th centuries. The hot mineral springs had also served as a health spot for the ancient Roman armies during their occupation of England.

Illus. 77. The popularity of hot-water bathing didn't begin with the hot tub. Archaeologists have discovered the oldest Roman public baths still in existence in the ruins of Pompeii.

The Roman Emperor Caracalla built a bathhouse in the third century A.D. that became known as the granddaddy of them all. It was huge, covering nearly 28 acres (11 hectares), and could handle 1,600 bathers at one time. Private baths were scattered throughout the building, and gardens, huge pools, and hundreds of rooms used for massage and oil rubdowns abounded. The Baths of Caracalla soon became a center of Roman social life, with emperors and the wealthy in attendance on a steady basis. However, it was also in the Baths of Caracalla that the infamous Roman orgy had much of its origin. Sometime after the opening of the baths, mixed bathing was legalized in Rome, and the libido of the bathers took over from there. Caracalla became known as a center for promiscuity, a retreat from the morals of the street, where a bather could submerge himself or herself not only in hot water, but in any type of pleasure he or she desired. The Baths of Caracalla became synonymous with the decline and fall of the Roman Empire (476 A.D.) and have often been cited as an example of ultimate Roman degeneracy.

105

When the Roman Empire fell, so did bathing as a cultural phenomenon within Western civilization. The Roman genius for architectural engineering allowed them to construct their successful bathing emporiums with intricate aqueducts and conduits, and they enjoyed their new toys with typical Roman enthusiasm. However, when their civilization fell, so did much of their knowledge and engineering proficiency. It would take what was left of Western civilization a long time to reconstruct a bathing system of comparable grandeur.

The Dark Ages (Middle Ages—beginning 476 A.D.) were not only dark, but veritably dry. The reaction of the Christians against the Roman sense of morality led to the eventual condemnation of bathing as a morally illicit practice that could only lead to absolute degeneration. The Christians pointed to the legendary orgies of the Roman bathhouses as evidence enough of the evils of bathing. Water itself became something of an illicit substance, thought to be a product of the devil that caused normally moral people to act in a highly immoral manner. During the reign of the clergy, many saints, such as Saint Benedict and Saint Jerome, lectured about the sins of bathing. They proselytized not only against public bathhouses, or communal bathing, but against everyday hygienic bathing. The clergy denied hot water and the medical and mental benefits of bathing to the masses, and to themselves. Even the liberal Pope, Gregory I (540–604 A.D.), allowed bathing only once a week.

Bathing flourished in the East at this time, especially within the growing Islamic Empire. During his initial years of rule, Muhammad (570–632 A.D.), the founder of Islam, had condemned the licentious activities of the Arabian tribes he had conquered. But, as Muhammad's Empire spread to the East and gained control of diverse populations, he began to relax many of his strict edicts. The Koran was structured in such a way as to gradually bring back some of the more acceptable practices which Muhammad had originally condemned, and one of those was bathing. Within the Islamic Empire, bathing became a highly structured and pleasurable ritual, with accompanying traditions and rules that the bather had to adhere to. The baths which were built during the rise of the Islamic Empire were beautifully decorated, incorporating an architectural sophistication that equaled that of Rome.

The Crusaders (11th–13th centuries A.D.) brought the Turkish baths back to Western civilization, along with the Eastern bathing rituals they had discovered during their travels, and the baths became an overnight success when they were introduced in Europe. But, upon their introduction into Western civilization, the baths also became centers of degeneracy and licentiousness. In England, the Turkish bath was little more than a brothel, an excuse for a man to disrobe and receive the attentions of a very willing masseuse. The Islamic precepts of bodily cleanliness and health were lost upon the libidinous bathers of the West.

The 14th and 15th centuries became notorious for their baths, and the promiscuity that existed therein. Turkish baths were continually being closed by the governments, and private bathing replaced them. Private baths were usually taken in a wooden or ceramic tub, with an attendant pouring warm water over the bathers. Often, these tubs were extremely large and could accommodate up to ten people. Communal bathing made sense in that it was difficult to keep large amounts of water warm. Many of the bathers during this time actually wore their clothes when taking a bath, yielding to propriety even though the intent of the bath more often than not was to revel in food, drink, and sex.

The Renaissance (14th–17th centuries A.D.) brought with it a revolutionary attitude towards bathing. Leonardo Da Vinci began designing luxurious bathrooms for royalty. These bathrooms were beautiful in style, and have become landmarks of design and splendor. They were built for at least two people, with huge tubs and exquisite accommodations. In many ways, the bathrooms built during the Renaissance in Europe represent the heights of bathing splendor.

The Industrial Revolution (late 18th century) brought about an entirely new attitude towards bathing that has remained with us to this day. Personal cleanliness became of great importance as a result of medical findings which linked lack of personal hygiene to disease and illness. As science progressed in its understanding of the human body, so did society in its desire to keep that body clean. With the Industrial Revolution came the singular bathtub and the shower. These were efficient means of cleansing the body in privacy, without ritual or tradition to accompany the process, and they were available to the common man. Bathing became an everyday routine that possessed all the romance and luxury of brushing one's teeth. Bathtubs were designed to accommodate only one person at a time, and with the efficiency of gas heating to warm the water, there was little need for communal bathing. Efficiency soon became the byword with which Western society regarded bathing.

During the 19th and early 20th centuries, medicinal baths began to flourish. These famous spas, such as the ones at Baden-Baden in Germany and Bath in England, lured health-seekers from all over the world to partake of the hot mineral springs. Health enthusiasts claimed that the minerals, plus the hot swirling waters, rejuvenated the body, curing every-

107

Illus. 78. The famous spa at Baden-Baden in Germany lured 19th and early 20th-century health-seekers from all over the world to partake of its hot mineral waters.

thing from rheumatism to old age. At the same time, the Turkish bath and the sauna grew in popularity, without the stigma of moral degeneracy that had surrounded their existence during the Medieval period. However, as in Grecian times, partaking of the baths at such places as Baden-Baden was expensive, limited to the wealthy. The ritual and social pleasures of bathing had yet to seep down to the working classes. So the average man found himself limited to his private daily bath or shower.

108

(Above) Illus. 79. Partaking of the baths at spas such as Baden-Baden in Germany was an expensive social privilege limited to the wealthy. (Below) Illus. 80. Elaborate complexes, housing famed medicinal baths, began to flourish in the 19th and early 20th centuries. High society met, mingled, and enjoyed the rejuvenating effects of the hot, swirling mineral waters which were claimed to cure everything from rheumatism to old age.
Shown here is Bad Nauheim in Germany.

In Japan, bathing took on a truly democratic flavor. The Japanese had long cherished the rituals of bathing, and considered the taking of the bath a most healthful and pleasurable social affair. In many private homes, the Japanese constructed wooden tubs capable of holding the entire family, or friends and guests. The waters were heated to the extreme limits of human endurance, often up to 120°F. (48°C.). The private tub in a Japanese home became the center of social and business life. Meetings were rarely held until the parties involved first submerged themselves in the scalding water, and then enjoyed a massage and a plunge into a cold pool. The Japanese obviously believe in soothing the body and soul before settling down to the rigors of negotiation.

The public baths in Japan are available to those people who do not have a private bath or tub in their home. These huge emporiums of pleasure are centers of the average citizen's social life. In these baths, an entire Japanese family can enjoy an afternoon or evening of massage, hot-water bathing, and good fellowship. The baths are open to everyone, and there is very little attention paid to privacy. Some of the bathhouses even have portholes through which passersby on the street can view the bathers. Segregation of the sexes in the Japanese baths is traditional, with very few of them allowing men and women to bathe together. There are, however, many retreats and spas throughout Japan that cater specifically to sexually integrated bathing. These luxurious spas feature incredibly beautiful settings, overnight accommodations and plenty of hot- and cold-water pools. It is in these retreats that the art of Japanese bathing has reached its pinnacle.

The Japanese public baths were, in fact, the forerunners of the modern American hot tub. During the 1950's and 1960's, many Westerners came in contact with the ritual of the Japanese bath, and the stories these travelers brought back to the United States served to whet the appetites of millions of people for the luxuries of these baths. Jacuzzis® and spas became extremely popular during the 1960's in the United States, and they became affordable to the average American as technology and the use of plastics brought the prices down. Americans were discovering what other people throughout the world had known for centuries—that swirling hot water is pleasurable, healthful, and an ingenious way of socializing. Millions of people began installing these hot-water pools as adjuncts to their swimming pools and as separate bathing areas in their homes.

The wooden hot tub, however, developed a following of its own. Legend has it that the first wooden hot tubs were put into use by a mellow group of people living in the mountains above Santa Barbara, California, during the 1960's. These people used old wine vats which they

Illus. 81. The Japanese consider the taking of the bath a most healthful and pleasurable social affair. In public baths such as this one, family and friends can enjoy an afternoon or evening of massage, hot-water bathing, and good company.

purchased cheaply from local wineries. The buyers took the vats apart, numbered the staves and floorboards, and then reassembled them on the property of the proud owner. Using a wide variety of pumps and heaters, these hot-tub pioneers began improving on their wooden tubs by introducing hydrojets and other accessories. The old wine vats became instantly popular with the mountain folk around Santa Barbara. Californians are always ready for unique and intriguing ways to enjoy themselves, and word of the "tub" soon began spreading up and down the California coast. The hot tub surfaced quickly among those who sought not only health and the invigorating effects of the hot waters, but also among those who were continually seeking subtle ways of getting their friends to take off their clothes. The hot-tub culture in California had begun.

The success of the early hot tubs extended far beyond the parameters of being a trend. The hot tub, essentially, was a reasonable and environmentally sound answer to the Jacuzzi and the spa. The wood of the

Illus. 82. An adaptation of the home spa or indoor hot tub, this indoor grotto creates a natural, peaceful atmosphere that would make a charming hot-tub setting.

Illus. 83. The solid wood of the tub blends naturally into the outdoor surroundings of trees, rocks, and shrubbery.

tub added an aspect of naturalness and comfort that was missing from the Jacuzzis and spas. The cost of installing a tub or building one's own was within almost everyone's reach, whereas Jacuzzis and spas were decidedly expensive. And, the social life inherent within the ritual of hot-tub bathing was somehow more appealing to people than that offered by the Jacuzzi and the spa.

Industries that produced reassembled hot-tub kits began flourishing in southern California, and their markets spread throughout the United States. Today, many such companies are doing a landmark business. Hot tubs are relatively inexpensive to operate, and many people, conscious of the rising cost of fuel and the exorbitant costs of installing a swimming pool, are turning to hot tubs as a viable option.

The popularity of the hot tub represents mankind's age-old desire to enjoy its bathing. Human beings have an instinct to socialize in a secure and comfortable environment, to rekindle that closeness that existed ages ago when people would huddle throughout the long, dark night around a bright, warm fire. Hot tubs provide people with that feeling of a totally

113

enjoyable and pleasurable experience that combines the best of socializing with the best of health.

The proliferation of hot tubs gives evidence to the fact that bathing as a communal ritual has finally come to the United States. It is an experience that is available to almost everyone, no matter what their status or income. More and more people are discovering why there were such great flourishes of communal bathing throughout history. They are learning the secret pleasures of sharing hot water with friends, or with a special acquaintance.

Hot-Tub Kits

If, after thinking it all over, you decide to take the easy way out, do not despair. Many other people have made the same decision, as a result of lack of time, skills, or a combination thereof. The easy way, then, is to take a Saturday afternoon and visit a local hot-tub dealer and buy your tub in kit form. These kits come with pre-cut staves, floors, hoops, and plumbing systems, and a complete guide to putting it all together. Of course, there are professionals at each store who, for a fee, would be happy to assemble the whole thing for you.

If you buy a pre-cut kit, and plan to assemble it yourself, you are saving the steps of cutting and bevelling the staves, cutting the floorboards, and making the benches. Otherwise, many of the steps will be the same as though you had made the tub from scratch. I highly recommend a kit if you have doubts about your skills as a cooper. In that case, you should have someone from the shop come out and install your tub and plumbing.

In California, one of the largest and most successful manufacturers of hot tubs is California Cooperage. Their factory is located in the town of San Luis Obispo, some 250 miles (400 km) north of Los Angeles. California Cooperage deals through a large chain of distributors and mail-order programs, thus making their tubs available to everyone. They provide with the pre-cut kit an instruction manual on how to assemble your tub, and they also include basic information about the systems available for plumbing, and tips on how best to use them.

A unique hot-tub company is now operating in Santa Barbara, California. It is called The Hot Tub Store and is run by Bruce Hanna and his brother Duane, who also operates the Village Pool Supply in the same location. Bruce Hanna came to California from the University of Illinois, where he was a professor, and instantly fell in love with the hot-tub scene then flourishing on the west coast. Bruce befriended the original hot-tub aficionados and soon began installing his own tubs. Hanna's claims to fame are his unique designs for hot-tub environments, many of which can be found in the palatial homes in and around Santa Barbara.

When I spoke with Hanna, he told me that his goal is to become a travelling designer, installing ready-made tubs and designing the perfect environments for those tubs throughout the country. Hanna will ship anywhere in the United States, and will also design a decking and plumbing system for your particular location. To use Hanna's unique facility, send specifications of your yard along with your order to Hanna, and he'll get in touch and work out the details. The address is: Bruce Hanna, The Hot Tub Store, 1080 Coast Village Rd., Santa Barbara, California 93103. (Phone: 805-969-4747). In Santa Barbara, Hanna's reputation is second to none. And considering Santa Barbara is the birthplace of hot tubs, that's saying a lot.

Costs for a kit will vary according to inflation and where you live. As of Spring, 1980, California Cooperage was selling a complete kit for $2,385. This includes a 4-foot high (1.22-m) tub with a 5-foot (1.52-m) diameter, including staves, floor joists, hoops, and all hardware; a one-horsepower Noryl pump with timer and filters; an electric spa heater; a four-jet hydro-massage unit; and enough piping and hardware to complete your assembly. California Cooperage is a highly reputable and reasonably priced dealer, so you can assume that their prices are about average.

Regarding your warranty with a company such as California Cooperage: the standard procedure is for the dealer to transfer the manufacturer's warranty to you, or, if that is less than a year, to guarantee coverage up to a full year.

Every company, of course, has a different program and a varied set of machinery which they use. Just be certain that the wood you buy is clear and kiln-dried. California Cooperage offers tubs made out of redwood, cedar, or mahogany—all of which work well.

It seems to me that purchasing a kit would make sense only if the tub were assembled and put into working order by a professional. I suggest checking with your dealer prior to laying down your money, to make sure that they have a qualified installer on hand. Otherwise, why not save money and simply have a professional cut your staves and floor and then assemble the tub by yourself?

Whether you choose to build, or buy a kit, once your hot tub is in working order, you're in for an adventure unlike any other. Enthusiasts provide a simple and direct formula for success for those about to embark on the hot-tub experience:

RELAX AND ENJOY!!

Appendix

HOT-TUB MANUFACTURERS

The following is a list of hot-tub manufacturers now operating:

Aquaponics
22135 Ventura Blvd.
Woodland Hills, California 91364

California Cooperage
Box E,
San Luis Obispo, California 93401
(805) 544-9300
1-800-549-6084

California Hottub
60 Third Ave
New York, New York 10003
(212) 982-3000

Gordon and Grant
423 North Quarantina
Santa Barbara, California 93103

Redwood in the Round Hot Tubs
125 Main St.
Westport, Connecticut 06880
(203) 226–3063

Santa Barbara Hotub Co.
41 Mountain Dr
Santa Barbara, California 93103

Sierra Hot Tubs
P.O. Box 1024
Tuolumne, California 95379

Sundown Hot Tubs
696 North Ohioville Rd
New Paltz, New York 12561

The Tubmakers
2500 Market St
Oakland, California 94607

SOLAR ENERGY DESIGNS

American Solar Energy Systems
4871 Topanga Canyon Blvd.
Woodland Hills, California 91364
(213) 884-1800

ENERGY-EFFICIENT SYSTEMS

Energy Management Consultants
4871 Topanga Canyon Blvd.
Woodland Hills, California 91364

BIBLIOGRAPHY

Hot Tubs, Leon Elder. Vintage Books, 1978.
Hot Tubs, Spas & Home Saunas, Editors of Sunset. Lane Pub, 1979.
Sensual Water, Barber & Levy. Contemporary Books, 1978.

Index